Written by
Gary O'Hanlon

Produced by
Bluebird Care

First published in Ireland in 2014
by Bluebird Care Ireland
www.bluebirdcare.ie

Edited by Joanne Sweeney Burke, Media Box

Typeset in Bembo and Avenir

Design and Project Management by Media Box
www.mediabox.ie

Printed and bound by GPS

ISBN: 978-0-9930131-0-2

Acknowledgements

Let me start by thanking the wonderful Joanne Sweeney-Burke of Media Box, without whom I would never have met Brian MacGoey, Managing Director and Eddie O'Toole, Operations Director of Bluebird Care. Without doubt Joanne has been the driving force behind this project and along with her trusted partners in crime Tom and Janine there would be nothing to read as they were always there at the end of the phone or email to wake me up and ensure I hit my deadlines.

Above: Gary pictured with Broadcaster George Hook and Joanne Sweeney-Burke. Photo Credit, Frances Muldoon Photography

To Brian, Eddie and the rest of the Bluebird Care team, thank you for the opportunity to write this book and to be a part of an incredible organisation.

To James and Beryl Kearney, thank you for the use of the magnificent Viewmount House grounds and kitchen which we used for the majority of the dish photography.

To Wojtek Manka, a great Chef and friend who gave up his valuable time off to come help me cook, test and taste all the dishes you see within the book. His speed, hard work and organisational skills made the task much easier, so thanks Chef.

To the amazing and extremely talented Harry Weir. I first worked on a photo shoot with Harry a few years ago for Food & Wine Magazine and I swore to myself if anyone ever asked me to write them a cookbook then Harry was going to be my number one choice to capture it. A true pro and a gentleman. Even when I decided on a whim that we had to drive to Donegal for two photographs Harry's response was instant "no problem". Thank you Harry.

To JP and Mark of Evolve Menswear, Letterkenny who provided the clothing for the photoshoot and videography.

To my wee wife Netty. I ignored all my "wee jobs" (I don't think they're wee jobs by the way) around the house for months as I was too busy on the keyboard putting the book together. I'm not going to say she was ok with me ignoring them, she still made me do them but we'll thank her anyway because, well, life's too short not to be doing what your wife tells you and we can't leave her out.

Contents

bluebird care

Foreword

Food for the Soul is a cookbook with you in mind. As a company we work with thousands of families every day. We care for people in their own home and in their community and so we become part of their every day, of their every week.

We wanted to give something back to individuals, families and communities and so we decided to publish a cookbook that provided healthy and wholesome recipes that you would enjoy cooking.

Many people cook as a hobby, as a way to relax or as a way of entertaining family and friends. However and wherever you use this cookbook, we hope you enjoy it.

We asked our resident food blogger, chef Gary O'Hanlon to come on board with us.

Gary tells a great story in his cooking and you will see this throughout every recipe in Food for the Soul.

A donation from each book sale will go to Active Retirement Ireland, one of our charity partners. They have over 500 Active Retirement Associations nationwide comprising 23,000 members. ARI advocates for retired people and they organise activities and oversee projects, which enable their members to live full and active lives in their communities.

We intend to bring our recipes to life with online videos and a series of nationwide cookery demonstrations so stay tuned to our website www.bluebirdcare.ie for more details.

You can send your feedback via email to info@bluebirdcare.ie or send a hand-written note to Bluebird Care Head Office, Riverfront, Howley's Quay, Limerick.

Eddie O'Toole
Operations Director

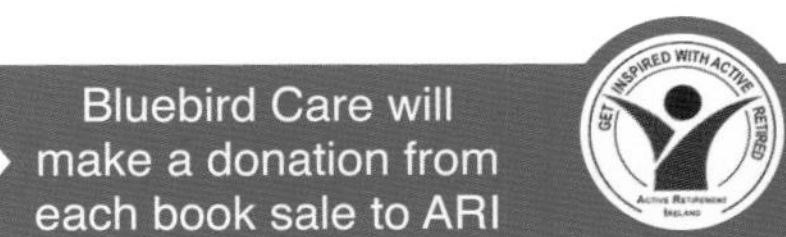

About Gary O'Hanlon

Gary O'Hanlon is Head Chef at award-winning VM Restaurant at Viewmount House in Co. Longford. Gary's career spans continents and includes many national awards and accolades, most recently the Georgina Campbell "Best Restaurant in Ireland" Award 2014. He has also entertained us with his culinary talents and big personality on TV in Ireland.

Gary cooked in Devlin's Restaurant in Boston before returning to Ireland in 2008. He then discovered Viewmount House and VM Restaurant where he has worked as Head Chef since.

The restaurant has been a massive success and has had a number of industry accolades including:

- Irish Independent, one of "Ireland's Top 10 Places to Stay & Eat"
- Bridgestone Top 100 Restaurant & Places to Stay Guide since 2010
- Food & Wine Magazine "Commended" Best Restaurant in Leinster 2011
- RAI Best Hotel Restaurant Leinster 2013
- Georgina Campbell "Sunday Lunch of the Year" Award 2012
- Georgina Campbell "Best Restaurant in Ireland" Award 2014

Gary is a member of Eurotoques Ireland and is a regular on our screens in shows such as RTE's Four Live, MasterChef Ireland, The Restaurant, The Today Show and TV3's Late Lunch Live.

His passion for food, locally sourced ingredients and for a new challenge attracted Bluebird Care to Gary and hence the partnership on Food for the Soul.

For more log onto: www.viewmounthouse.com

An Introduction from Gary O'Hanlon

I really enjoyed writing this cookbook which is aimed at those of you who love good wholesome and traditional food but with a modern twist. Partnering with Bluebird Care has been a really exciting project for me.

This is in fact my very first published cookbook and I am thrilled that you are part of it. I have tested and tasted and prepped and prepared every recipe with you in mind.

As an introduction to Food for the Soul, I offer you some of my cooking tips about how to get the best from this cookbook. I hope you enjoy cooking my recipes as much as I have enjoyed writing and photographing them with Harry Weir.

This cookbook is accompanied by a nationwide series of cookery demonstrations and a suite of online videos which bring my cooking to life. Log onto www.bluebirdcare.ie for more details.

Happy cooking!

Chef Gary

Key to Symbols

EASY COOKING INDEX

Easy

Moderate

Challenging

Coeliac Friendly

Vegetarian

Healthy Option

Freezable

Handy Tips

READ

Read through your chosen recipe in advance.

SHOPPING LIST

Put together a little shopping list and you'll be in and out of the shop in no time. This will save you time scrounging around the back of store cupboards in search of ingredients you more than likely don't have. It's also wise to hit the shops with a controlled and organised shopping list. This way you will not spend money on things you may already have.

PREPARE AHEAD

When it comes to cooking any of the dishes make sure you have most of the groundwork done. For example have your potatoes peeled, leaves washed and everything measured.

USE THE 'HOW TO GUIDE'

The more difficult dishes have been photographed in stages for your benefit. We've called this the "How To Guide." Make sure to use them. I find that seeing things in pictures can really help.

BE ORGANISED

Keep all of your ingredients close by once you start cooking. Have all your seasonings on the same tray or plate. For example, if you are using salt, pepper, spices, sugar or other seasonings have them close by each other because the chances are you'll forget one. So by thinking ahead you won't end up adding seasoning too late nor will you begin with a vital ingredient missing from your cupboard.

TIME

Allow plenty of time if you're not used to cooking and you're using the book as a reason to try. The recipes are all achievable once you follow them correctly but give yourself plenty of time and enjoy yourself.

Practice makes perfect and as I always say in Viewmount House, "Don't worry about speed until you get the quality of the finished product right first." Speed will come naturally so don't put yourself under pressure and have fun.

PLANNING

If you're using the book to create a little dinner party be sure to think ahead and use the 1-3 guide. 1 being the easiest and 3 the slightly more challenging.

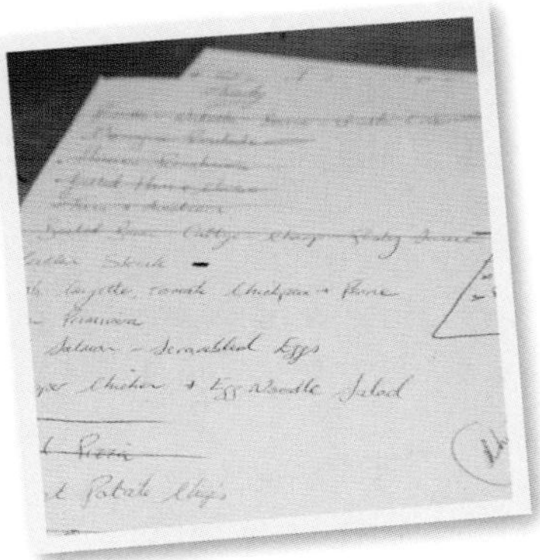

Stick to a dessert that's made in advance - my option would be the Berrymisiu – or maybe pick out a main course that cooks low and slow in the oven – perhaps Lamb Shoulder - and opt for a starter that can also be prepared well in advance - like the Duck Leg Confit.

This way you leave plenty of time to mingle with your family or friends.

As you get stronger and more comfortable in the kitchen you can start to rock out anything and everything but the key for me is to never bite off more than you can chew (pun intended). I want you to enjoy cooking and there are plenty of recipes inside to help you do just that.

SEASONING

When adding seasonings always add a little at a time. You can always add more but it's virtually impossible to take it out without ruining a dish or altering the consistency.

My measurements are merely a guide. You may prefer more salt or none at all - it's absolutely no problem. I add a little salt here and there but if you don't consume salt, play around with herbs and before long you'll have a nice balance of flavour. It's all about trial and error.

You've got to make mistakes to reach perfection!

AVOID CLUTTER

Have only one knife at a time on your chopping board. You can only use one at a time and having more lying around is only going to get in your way and quite possibly cause you to cut yourself.

Also, as soon as you're finished using a utensil, put it in the sink or into the dishwasher out of your way. Keep a clutter free counter top and chopping board and you'll have the space needed to see what you're doing.

SAFETY

Be careful if you're cooking with hot oil. For example, when cooking the fish cakes be sure to use a deep fat fryer with a controlled thermostat. Heating oil in a pot over an open flame is extremely dangerous and I don't recommend it.

Whilst cooking, make sure the handles of all your pots and pans are facing in and not pointing out towards you. It's very easy to catch a stray handle and cause injury so please be careful.

Make sure to turn off all gas/electric when you're finished cooking. Create a little checklist and it will only take you a minute to glance through it when you're done cooking. Sometimes amidst the excitement of finishing a lovely meal it's easy to sit down and revel in your hard work but if an oven, for example, isn't working on a timer and is quite silent it's very easy to head off to bed with it still on. So try to get into the habit of checking everything. We do this at the restaurant every night.

EQUIPMENT

Invest in a couple of nice pots if you don't already have some. A few good solid pots are all you need along with a heavy based non-stick frying pan.

You'll find me making many references to a heavy based non-stick frying pan. It'll prove to be a good purchase. Just remember to clean with a soft cloth or sponge, never use metal scrubbers otherwise you'll damage the Teflon and whenever you place into a cupboard place one or two paper towels on the Teflon so other pots and pans can't damage the non-stick surface.

Invest in one or two good sharp knives - a chopping knife, carving knife and a little chef's knife or paring knife, as some call them.

Scales are important, especially when it comes to baking or making desserts.

A nice chopping board is essential. I prefer wooden or plastic boards to glass. Food items can slip quite easily on glass boards so for that reason I find them too dangerous.

Always remember to enjoy yourself.

A good chef is a clean chef and a happy chef always produces tastier food.

Enjoy and thank you for taking time to read, and cook dishes from, Food for the Soul.

Chef Gary

Breakfast

What is breakfast? For me it's generally a baguette and two bananas whilst zipping around the place. I hate to admit it but it's the one meal I tend to always pass. Always too busy, rushing here and there and always in a hurry. It drives my wife, wee Netty, crazy.

Our first baby, wee Cora O'Hanlon was born on New Year's Eve (2013) and I'm on a promise to mend my ways and get myself into a proper routine of cooking breakfast.

Saturday's though are different. Netty is off work, she's a schoolteacher, and she just loves pancakes for breakfast. I'm more of a savoury type of guy so I'll rustle Netty up her favourite dish of Pancakes, Vanilla Bean Cream, Berries and Maple Syrup (see Page 22). Meanwhile, I'll throw together an omelette or some of Ernan McGettigan's gorgeous sausages from Donegal Town.

Those types of mornings are magical. We sit, stuff our faces, laugh, play with Salty and Pepper, our wee pups, and life is great. It won't be long before little Cora gets to enjoy them also.

Why I can't do that every day is beyond me? But I guess it's the fact that during the week I'm on my own for breakfast as Netty is working and so I don't feel up to putting in the effort for myself. It's a shame really.

For those of you that are like Netty and love making breakfast get stuck into some of the recipes in the following chapter.

You won't be disappointed.
Happy cooking!

Chef Gary

HAVEN SMOKEHOUSE "TURF" SMOKED SALMON

with Scrambled Eggs

Ingredients

3 slices turf or oak-smoked salmon

2 chives

3 eggs

30ml cream

2 knobs butter

SERVES 1

Method

Break the three eggs into a bowl and mix with a fork.

Season with a little salt and white pepper. Add the cream.

Heat the butter in a heavy based non-stick pot on a low heat.

Add in the egg mix and mix until scrambled with a plastic spatula.

Take off the eggs about 1 minute before they are actually cooked
Keep stirring.

This way you'll have lovely soft scrambled eggs and they won't dry out.

Place the smoked salmon on a plate, spoon on the scrambled eggs and top with chopped chives.

Serve with some sourdough toast and Irish country butter.

In my mother's hometown of Carrigart in Co. Donegal, I recently came across a lovely couple who were "Turf" Smoking Salmon. Declan McConnellogue and Sue Cruse have set up a cracking little artisan food business and each week Declan makes the short journey over to Marine Harvest in Fanad where he hand picks his Salmon and then swings back over Mulroy Bay and sets to work creating this uniquely flavoured smoked salmon. It's early days yet but I predict many great things from these guys. For those lucky enough to be anywhere near Donegal you can buy the Salmon at Harry's Food Market on Saturday mornings in Bridgend. For those of you further afield I'm sure it's only a matter of time before it starts popping up in your area. In the meantime just use any type of Irish Smoked Salmon you can find. The country is blessed with some of the best smokers in the world from Sally Barnes and John Rogan to Frank Hedderman and Brigitta Curtin so I'm sure you'll find one you love.

Inset: Anne, Gary's Mum

MUSHROOM & SPINACH OMELETTE

Ingredients

2 eggs
20ml cream
4 mushrooms, sliced
50g spinach leaves
Salt and white pepper
50g grated mozzarella
2 tsp. olive oil

SERVES 1

Method

Heat a heavy based frying pan.

Crack the eggs into a bowl, season a little with salt and pepper.

Add the oil to the pan, then add the sliced mushrooms and cook until soft.

Now add the spinach and cook until it's wilted.

Mix the eggs with a fork and pour over the spinach and mushrooms.

Roll around the pan evenly.

Using a plastic spatula, lift up the edges and let the egg mix pour in.

Repeat until all the egg is cooked.

Add the cheese (or don't if you want to keep it healthier).

Using the spatula, slide it under the omelette and flick one half over on the other to give you a half moon effect.

Slide onto a plate and serve.

TURN PAGE FOR HOW-TO GUIDE →

I moved to Boston in September 1999 and one of my first jobs was in "The Kells of Boston" and every Sunday I, along with my good buddy Wee Joe, would work an omelette station for our 'All You Can Eat' brunch. Trust me when I tell you that we would easily churn out 200-plus omelettes each on a Sunday without fail.

Years later I moved on to Devlin's Restaurant, where I was to stay for the remainder of my time in the States. It was here I first added the mushroom and spinach omelette to the Brunch menu.

It was the most popular choice by miles and for good reason. A lovely flavour combination, I'm sure you'll all agree. To make this an even healthier option, leave out the cheese and use egg whites only. Use three eggs if making an egg white omelette though.

Inset:
Gary with his old boss Tom Devlin

MUSHROOM & SPINACH OMELETTE

How to GUIDE

STEP 1
Heat a heavy based frying pan.

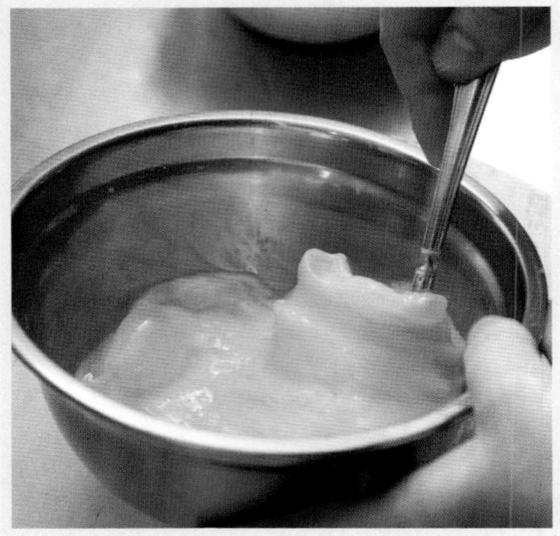

STEP 2
Crack the eggs into a bowl, season a little with salt and pepper.

STEP 3
Add the oil to the pan, then add the sliced mushrooms and cook until soft.

STEP 4

Now add the spinach and cook until it's wilted.

STEP 5

Mix the eggs with a fork and pour over the spinach and mushrooms. Roll around the pan evenly.

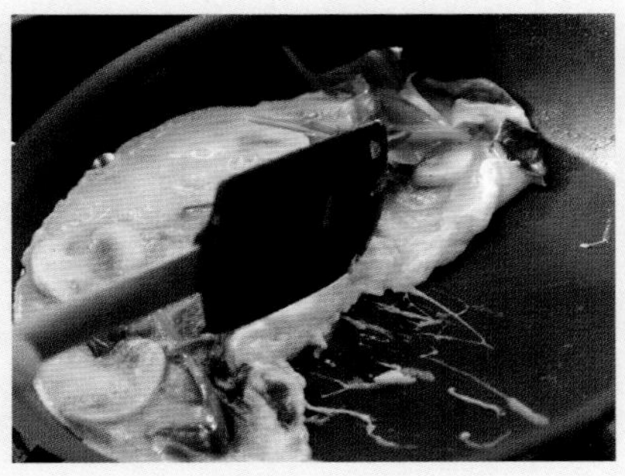

STEP 6

Using a plastic spatula, lift up the edges and let the egg mix pour in. Repeat until all the egg is cooked.

STEP 7

Add the cheese (if using).

STEP 8

Using the spatula, slide it under the omelette and flick one half over on the other to give you a half moon effect.

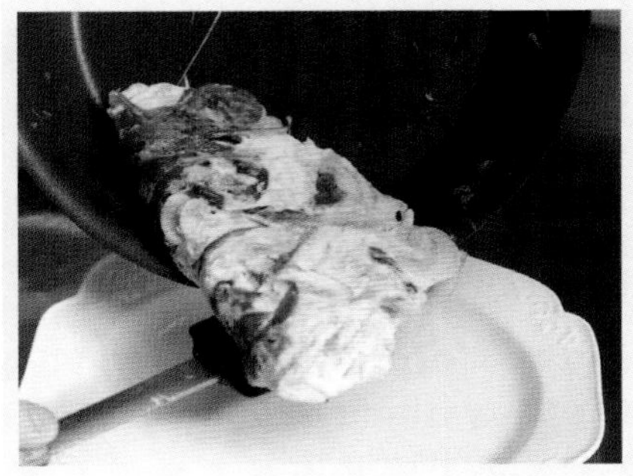

STEP 9

Slide onto a plate and serve.

PANCAKES with Berries, Vanilla Cream, Nutella & Maple Syrup

Ingredients

Berry Compote
10 raspberries
10 blueberries
10 blackberries
5 strawberries diced up
2 tsp. caster sugar

Pancake Batter
3 eggs
400ml full fat milk
100-200g of flour
100g caster sugar (you can add a little more if you prefer them sweeter but bear in mind we'll also be using sweetened cream and maple syrup)

For the Cream
250ml cream
2 tsp. icing sugar
A vanilla pod scraped out or 2-3 drops of vanilla essence

Method

Berry Compote
Mix everything together very slowly until the sugar dissolves and there's a lovely sheen to your berries. Set aside.

SERVES 2

Method - Cream
Add all the ingredients to a bowl and blend with an electric blender or by hand. It'll take a while longer to thicken if whisking by hand. Whisk until stiff.

Method - Pancake Batter
Whisk the eggs in a large bowl.
Add the sugar, whisk again until sugar dissolves.
Now add the milk and whisk to blend.
Add the flour bit by bit.
The flour quantity will differ from person to person. If, like me, you prefer them more crepe-like then use around 100g or if you prefer them slightly thicker add more.
The key is to add the flour in bit by bit.

Now to Cook
Heat the pan with approximately 10g of butter.
Do not let the butter brown.
Once melted swirl the butter around the base of the pan, this'll help prevent sticking.
Ladle one big scoop of pancake mix into the middle of the pan then swirl it to evenly distribute until the entire base of the pan is covered.
Cook on a medium heat until little bubbles appear. When it slides easily back and forth on the pan, it's ready for flipping.
Flip the pancake or put a flat spatula underneath and turn it.
Cook for a further 1-2 minutes then slide off onto a plate or chopping board.
Roll the pancake up. Place onto your plate.
Dust all over with icing sugar.
Spoon on the berries. Drizzle with maple syrup. Top with whipped cream and Nutella.

What You'll Need

1 10" or 12" non-stick pan
(the heavier the better)
1 bowl, 1 whisk
1 ladle, 1 sieve
10g of butter per pancake
A bottle of maple syrup
A jar of Nutella
A big plate to serve

This dish was one of my first blog posts for Bluebird Care so hopefully some of you have already tried it. If not, get cracking. This is one of Netty's favourite Saturday morning treats - although she'll argue she doesn't get them every Saturday. Worth waiting for though I say.

Inset: Gary's beautiful wife, Netty

GARY'S HUEVOS RANCHEROS

TIME TO 2 IMPRESS

Ingredients

6 eggs

6 10" flour tortillas

100g sliced jalapeños

1 red chilli

3 scallions

1 red pepper

1 green pepper

2 medium white onions

1 tin of chopped tomatoes

12 baby potatoes, cooked and cut into quarters

2 chorizo sausages

Half a bunch of coriander finely chopped

2 tsp. paprika

SERVES 6

Method

Slice and sauté the chorizo.

When almost cooked add the onion, jalapeños, sliced chilli and peppers.

Now add the cooked potato, paprika, season and continue to sauté.

In a large non-stick pan add the flour tortilla one by one and heat for approximately 15 seconds on each side. Repeat for the remaining tortillas.

Add the chopped tomatoes to the potato and chorizo mix. Bring to the boil, then simmer for 10-15 minutes.

Taste and adjust seasoning.

Add the flour tortilla to the base of a very large ovenproof dish.

Spoon on the potato and chorizo mix.

Now crack the eggs onto the mix leaving a space between each one.

Place in a pre-heated oven until the eggs cook.

Sprinkle with fresh coriander and scallions and serve family style.

My days off are almost always Mondays and Tuesdays. It was on one of my days off that I was in the car travelling home to Donegal. It was just after the US Presidential election and I was listening to our friend George Hook on Newstalk talking to Michael Graham, a radio presenter from Boston. As always the conversation was getting pretty heated. George was put out by Michael's breakfast choice of Huevos Rancheros and didn't shy away from giving Michael his thoughts on them. Having had the pleasure of cooking with George on RTE's The Restaurant I know he loves his food so I've decided to put a little Irish twist on Huevos Rancheros and let's hope big George gives them a whirl. This is a family style recipe and great for a weekend morning when family or friends are visiting. You can divide the recipe out for smaller numbers but the one here will serve approximately six adults.

Inset: George Hook,
Broadcaster and Author

BACON WRAPPED TERRINE
of Herterich's of Longford Black & White Pudding

Ingredients

800g Herterich's of Longford black pudding

800g Herterich's of Longford white pudding

2 chicken breasts

2 tsp. chopped thyme

2 whole eggs

2 egg whites

Salt and white pepper

10 slices bacon rashers

30ml cream

2 cups of fine breadcrumbs

SERVES 20 SLICES*

**approximate*

TOP TIPS

As a breakfast serve with poached egg and some spinach

As a main course, pan sear and serve with champ and sauce lyonnaise

Method

Blend the chicken in a food processor with the cream.
Season.
Add the herbs.
Add the eggs.
Blend until smooth and set aside.

Break up the black pudding and add to a mixer with a spade attachment.
Add half the chicken mousse.
Leave to mix for one minute then add enough breadcrumbs to dry and bind the mixture.
You want it dry but not too dry.
Slightly wet to the touch without sticking.

Repeat with the white pudding mix.

Line bread tins with cling film.
Now layer with overlapping slices of bacon.
Half fill with white pudding then top with the black mixture.
Fold over any over lapping pieces of bacon then fold over the cling film.
Now wrap the loaf tins approximately 6 times with cling film making sure it's air tight.
Place in a deep tray and fill with warm water ¾ of the way up the terrine.
Bake au bain marie for 1 hour and 20 minutes at 160°C.

Remove from the bain marie.
Leave to cool overnight.
Slice like a loaf and pan fry in Donegal rapeseed oil.

TURN PAGE FOR HOW-TO GUIDE →

I love black and white pudding. Who doesn't? For me though Louis Herterich in Longford Town makes the best in Ireland and I'm blessed that it's right on the doorstep of Viewmount House. Herterich's has been in business in the town since 1956. Originally opened by Louis' father Louis Senior, Louis Junior now has the reigns and he has continued on with the incredible methods, recipes and customer service instilled in him by his father. I wanted to combine both the black and white pudding and there's no better way than in a terrine, wrapped in bacon. Slice and serve as is, or pan fry and top with spinach, poached eggs and Hollandaise or use as a dinner and serve with mash, veg and onion gravy. Let your imagination go wild.

Inset: Louis Herterich with Gary
Photo by Paula Ryan Photography

BACON WRAPPED TERRINE
of Herterich's of Longford Black & White Pudding

STEP 1
Line bread tins with cling film.

STEP 2
Layer with overlapping slices of bacon.

STEP 3
Half fill with white pudding...

STEP 4

...then top with the black mixture.

STEP 5

Fold over any over lapping pieces of bacon...

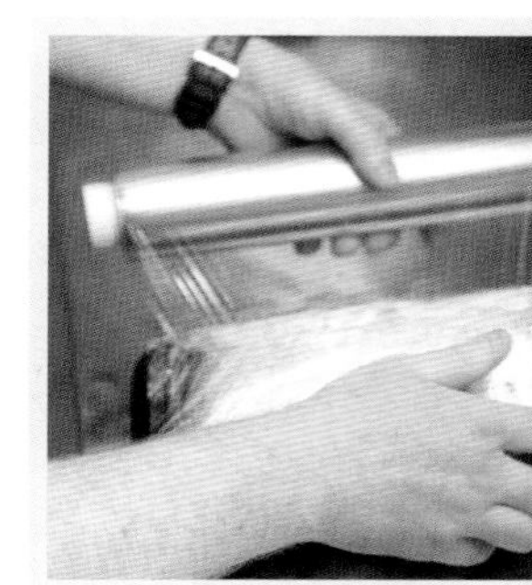

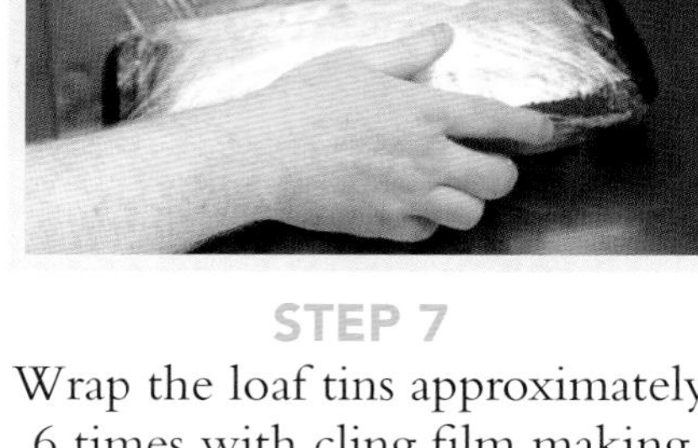

STEP 6

...then fold over the cling film.

STEP 7

Wrap the loaf tins approximately 6 times with cling film making sure it's air tight.

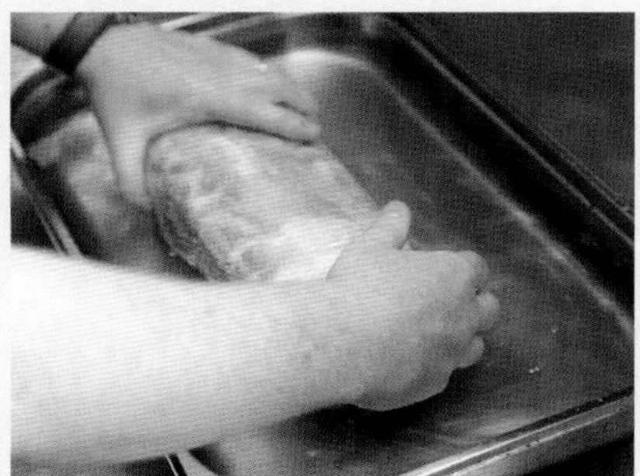

STEP 8

Place in a deep tray and fill with warm water ¾ of the way up the terrine. Bake au bain marie for 1 hour and 20 minutes at 160°C. Remove from the bain marie. Leave to cool overnight.

Snacks

This is the best chapter of the book.

Why you ask?

For me it's the diverse range of dishes and the fact that they are probably the easiest and fastest to prepare so I imagine that those of you who put this great book to good use will return to this chapter time and time again.

When you make the Chicken Quesadillas or the Naan Bread Pizza you'll be addicted. The first Christmas you make Pat's Meat Pie 'Tourtiere' I promise you, like it is for Pat and I, it'll become an annual tradition.

The gorgeous simple technique of buttering the outside of your grilled Ham & Cheese or Tuna & Sweetcorn Melt and cooking on a frying pan will change how you eat your Toasties forever. From the thick wholesome warming Cullen Skink to Netty's Favourite Chicken Salad, this chapter has something for everyone and every taste.

Happy cooking!

Chef Gary

TWICE BAKED POTATO with Chive, Horseradish & Crème Fraîche

Ingredients

1 large baker potato (Rooster baker)

2 tbspn. thick crème fraîche

2 tsp. finely sliced chives

Salt and pepper to taste

SERVES 1

Method

Bake the large rooster potato without foil for approximately 50-60 minutes at 170°C. Remove from the oven when a cocktail stick passes through the potato with ease.

Let rest for 10 minutes.
Now slice the cap off the potato lengthwise. Take approximately a quarter of the potato off the cap.

Using a spoon scoop the potato from the cap and place in a large bowl.
Set aside.
Now scoop the inside from the remaining potato being careful to leave a 1-2cm depth of potato on the inside.
You're basically creating a bowl from the baked potato and you want to leave just enough on the skin so that the potato can stand alone on a plate without falling in on itself.

Add the scooped out potato to the bowl with the potato from the cap.
Add all the remaining ingredients and season to taste.

Now spoon the mixture back into the hollowed out baked potato.
Pack it up loosely so as to give a pyramid effect then gently even it out towards the sides.

Place into a pre-heated oven at 180°C and bake until brown crispy edges appear (approximately 6 minutes).

Remove and serve with crisp garden leaves and a dollop of Aioli or garlic mayonnaise.

TURN PAGE FOR HOW-TO GUIDE →

I first tasted this when my old boss in Boston, Tom Devlin served it with a steak one night. It's a great idea and I think it adds a little bit of style and flavour to a boring old regular baked potato. You could also add some black pudding and top with a poached egg and serve it as a meal in its own right but I love it with a good steak.

TWICE BAKED POTATO
with Chive, Horseradish & Crème Fraîche

How to GUIDE

STEP 1
Cook the potato and let rest for 10 minutes.

STEP 2
Slice the cap off the potato lengthwise. Using a spoon scoop the potato from the cap and place in a large bowl. Set aside.

STEP 3

Now scoop the inside from the remaining potato being careful to leave a 1-2cm depth of potato on the inside. You're basically creating a bowl from the baked potato and you want to leave just enough on the skin so that the potato can stand alone on a plate without falling in on itself. Add the scooped out potato to the bowl with the potato from the cap.

STEP 4

Add all the remaining ingredients.

STEP 5

Season to taste.

STEP 6

Spoon the mixture back into the hollowed out baked potato. Pack it up loosely so as to give a pyramid effect then gently even it out towards the sides. Place into a pre-heated oven at 180°C and bake until brown crispy edges appear, approximately 6 minutes.

CHEESE BURGER SLIDERS
with Red Onion Mayonnaise & Cheddar

Ingredients

2 red onions

100g Cheddar

2 leaves of lettuce of choice

5 slices of tomato

5 tsp. mayonnaise

50ml red wine vinegar

3 tbsp. red currant jelly

1 tsp. Tabasco sauce

Burger Mix

25oz steak mince

4 tsp. Worcester sauce

2 tsp. Tabasco sauce

1 finely chopped onion

2 tsp. Heinz tomato ketchup

1 egg

100-120g fine breadcrumbs

SERVES 6-8*

**depending on how thick you want them*

Method

Onion Mayonnaise

Finely dice the red onion.
Sweat in a pot until soft.
Add the vinegar and reduce by half.
Now add 1 tsp. of Tabasco sauce and the redcurrant jelly.

Cook on a low heat until most of the juice has evaporated and the onions slightly caramelize.

Set aside to cool then mix in the mayonnaise with a spoon.

Burgers

Combine all the ingredients in a large bowl. If the mix is too wet add a little more breadcrumbs and likewise if it's too dry add a little more ketchup or an extra egg.

You'll know the mix is perfect when it doesn't stick to the edges of the bowl or your hands.

Mould the sliders out into 5oz patties and cook on a medium heat in a heavy based non-stick frying pan.

When ready add the cheese and let it melt.

Spoon the onion mayonnaise onto both sides of your hamburger bap, add a piece of lettuce, the tomato and finally the burger and the cap.

Stick a cocktail stick through the top and serve with the remaining onion mayonnaise.

TURN PAGE FOR HOW-TO GUIDE →

My very first blog post for Bluebird Care was on the horse meat scandal that sadly broke back in early 2013. I wrote about how easy it was to make a burger mixture without having to use store bought frozen burgers which, as it turns out, can have any amount of unknown ingredients in them. Go to your butcher and ask for good mince. The ratio you're looking for is 85% meat 15% fat. Don't worry about the fat content as most of it will render during the cooking process and as it trickles through the burger it's that little bit of fat that's going to flavour the burger. I've added a little twist here and used little sliders. You can create your own if you use the same recipe for my white bread. Simply cut off 15g balls of dough from the mix, then follow the proving stages and bake the same way as directed. They'll obviously cook that little bit quicker and they freeze really well so you can stock the freezer. Alternatively just buy the normal burger buns and make a 6oz burger.

CHEESE BURGER SLIDERS
with Red Onion Mayonnaise & Cheddar

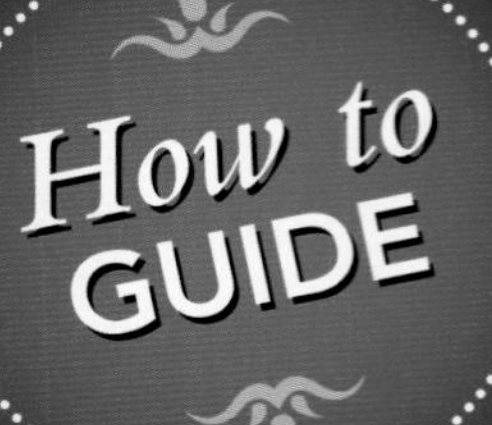

STEP 1

Combine all the ingredients in a large bowl.

STEP 2
If the mix is too wet add a little more breadcrumbs and likewise if it's too dry add a little more ketchup or an extra egg.

STEP 3
You'll know the mix is perfect when it doesn't stick to the edges of the bowl or your hands.

STEP 4
Mould the sliders out into 5oz patties.

STEP 5
Cook on a medium heat in a heavy based non-stick frying pan.

HAM HOCK & SPLIT PEA BROTH

Ingredients

2 ham hocks (soaked in cold water for 24 hours)

1 large onion finely chopped

100g barley soaked in cold water for 2 hours

100g green split peas

100g yellow split peas

3 carrots diced

4 stalks of celery, peeled then diced

5 litres chicken stock

1lb butter

2 cups flour

White pepper and salt to taste

Method

Boil the ham hocks for 3 hours or until the meat is falling from the bone.
Set aside.

Melt the butter and add the carrots, onion, celery, peas and barley.
Cook for 5 minutes stirring every minute.

Add the flour to make a roux.
Mix well but gently.
Now add the chicken stock.

Mix well and turn down to a very low heat.
Keep mixing every 5 minutes for 1 hour or until vegetables etc. are cooked.

Adjust consistency if it gets a little thick then season.

Rip off chunks of the ham hock and drop into the broth.

Will make approximately 15-20 bowls.

SERVES 15

TOP TIPS

The soup freezes well so don't be afraid to make the larger batch.

You could replace the ham hock with chicken by boiling a whole chicken, using the stock for the broth then ripping up the meat and dropping into the broth.

This is the perfect winter warmer broth. Ham Hock is still extremely cheap so this is very budget friendly. Sometimes you may not need to soak the ham hock in water overnight as they're not as salty as they once were. Again it all depends on how strong your butcher's cure is. Like everything else it's trial and error and you can decide if it's necessary after your first attempt whether you soak them or not.

ROAST SWEET POTATO & GINGER SOUP

Ingredients

4 medium to large peeled sweet potatoes

2 white onions

6 sprigs of thyme

1 finger of ginger

Salt and white pepper

4 chicken bouillon stock cubes

5 litres of water

100ml olive oil

SERVES 15

Method

Slice up the potatoes and add to a large roasting tray.

Add the onion, sliced ginger, thyme and season.

Add the oil and mix all the ingredients well.

Place into a pre-heated oven at 200°C and roast until the edges are well charred and the potatoes become golden.

Now add to a pot, cover with water and boil for 30 minutes.

Add the chicken stock cubes and blend with a hand blender.

Pass through a fine strainer, taste and season.

This recipe will serve approximately 15 people.

TOP TIPS

It freezes perfectly so add to 250ml airtight containers and freeze individually.
Add to a pot on a low heat whenever you want it.
Make sure to heat thoroughly though. Serve.

By simply roasting the sweet potatoes before making this soup you transform a beautiful soup into an incredible one. The subtle char that you get on the edges of the sweet potato add a fantastic depth of flavour and lasting taste to the soup. Use the same trick with potato soup, celeriac soup or even roast bell pepper. You'll be amazed at how much more flavour you can extract from the core ingredient.

CHICKEN QUESADILLA
with Sour Cream & Tomato Salsa

Ingredients

200g cooked chicken

2 10" flour tortillas

2 tsp. ground cumin

5 tbspn. chopped coriander

100g grated mozzarella cheese

2 tbspn. sour cream

3 tomatoes (diced)

½ red onion finely chopped

Juice of 1 lime

1 clove garlic (finely chopped)

5 tsp. olive oil

SERVES 2

Method

Mix the chicken, cheese, cumin and half of the coriander together in a bowl.

Lay out the two tortillas and divide the chicken mixture between the two but leaving half of each tortilla clear so as to allow you to fold one side over the other.

Rub each side with olive oil and gently cook on a non-stick pan turning carefully once you get a golden colour.

Place in a pre-heated oven at 180°C for 6 minutes.

When the quesadilla is in the oven combine the diced tomato with lime juice, chopped garlic, chopped red onion and the remaining coriander.

Season to taste and add olive oil. Season and taste again.

Remove the quesadilla from the oven, cut into quarters and serve with a ramekin of sour cream and a generous spoonful of the tomato salsa.

This dish is a South American favourite and one I first started making about 14 years ago in Boston. The cheese mix is pretty much the same as that of the Naan Bread Pizzas, which is in the book also, so if you make the mix why not try your hand at both. The cheese mix will last a few days in the fridge covered.

**Inset:
Gary and his Dad, John in Boston**

ROSE'S FISH CAKES
with Tartar Sauce

Ingredients

2 cooked potatoes
50g salmon
50g cod
50g plaice
30g smoked haddock
50g crab meat
1 leek
50g coriander
Juice of 1 lime
Juice of 1 lemon
Salt and pepper to taste

300g fine breadcrumbs
2 eggs
300ml milk
300g flour

Vegetable oil

6 tbsp. mayonnaise
30g gherkins
30g capers
Juice of 1 lime

**depending on cake size*

Method

Fish Cakes

Place all the fish on a baking tray and bake at 160°C for 6 minutes.
Add the cooked fish to the potatoes.

Sweat the leek without colour in a little oil.
Add to the potatoes and fish.
Add the lemon and lime juice along with the coriander.

Season to taste.

Mix the eggs and milk together.
Put the egg wash, flour and breadcrumbs into three separate bowls.

Now mould the fish cakes between your hands.
It'll make between 6 and 8 fish cakes.

Pass through the flour, then egg wash then the breadcrumbs.

Heat a heavy based frying pan with a little vegetable oil and cook until golden on each side, then place the pan into the oven for 4-6 minutes at 160°C .

Tartar Sauce

Whilst in the oven chop up the gherkins and capers.
Mix through the mayonnaise and add the lime juice.
Season to taste.

Serve the fish cake with a dollop of tartar sauce and some dressed salad.

I probably shouldn't say I have a favourite customer but I do. Rose Cunningham is our next door neighbour here at Viewmount House and I can't remember a Sunday lunch that Rose has missed in our first six years of business.
Regardless of what I put on the menu Rose has fish cakes for her starter. It doesn't matter if they're on the menu or not. If Rose is in for lunch, Rose gets her fish cakes. She's going to be a little mad with me though as I've made just one fishcake in this recipe as opposed to two smaller ones, which is how Rose likes them. I'm sure she'll forgive me.

Inset: Gary with Rose

NAAN BREAD PIZZA
with Basil Pesto, Chicken, Mozzarella & Cumin Fresh Tomato Salsa

Ingredients

4 naan bread

1 cooked breast of chicken, diced up

4 tbspn. basil pesto

400g grated mozzarella cheese

2 tbspn. ground cumin

100g fresh coriander

Tomato Salsa

4 ripe tomatoes quartered and core removed

50g coriander

Juice of one lime

Olive oil to bind

Salt and pepper to taste

1 red onion diced

Cherry Pepper Mayonnaise

6 spoons heavy mayonnaise

4 peppadew (cherry) peppers

SERVES 4

Method

In a large bowl add the chicken, cheese, chopped fresh coriander and cumin together and mix well.

Add a large spoon of the basil pesto to the base of the naan bread and spread to the edges.

Sprinkle on even amounts of the cheese and chicken mixture.

Place on a tray in a pre-heated oven at 170°C for approximately 6 minutes or alternatively set on the cooler side of a pre-heated BBQ, close the lid and cook for 4-6 minutes, checking every 1-2 minutes.

Whilst the naan pizza is cooking combine the tomatoes, onion, coriander and lime juice together in a bowl. Season to your taste with salt and pepper. Drizzle in olive oil to your required taste to create a salsa.

For the cherry pepper mayonnaise just blend the ingredients together until smooth in a food processor.

Remove the naan bread from the oven.

Cut into slices and serve with spoons of the fresh tomato salsa and a generous spoonful of the cherry pepper mayonnaise.

This dish is also lovely with a spoon of store bought guacamole, sour cream or natural yoghurt.

They always say you should keep your mother-in-law happy and this is why this recipe is featured in the book. Netty's mammy Bernie is a keen cook herself and loves to get stuck into baking and her Beef Stew is 100% the best I've ever tasted. But during a summer BBQ at her house I came up with this wee beauty and it became an instant hit. Now we spark up the BBQ in any kind of weather just so we can enjoy this wee cracker.

Inset: Bernie, Gary's mother-in-law

How to GUIDE

NAAN BREAD PIZZA
with Basil Pesto, Chicken, Mozzarella

STEP 1
In a large bowl add the chicken, cheese, chopped fresh coriander and cumin together and mix well.

STEP 2
Add a large spoon of the basil pesto to the base of the naan bread and spread to the edges.

STEP 3

Sprinkle on even amounts of the cheese and chicken mixture. Place on a tray in a pre heated oven at 170°C for approximately 6 minutes or alternatively set on the cooler side of a pre-heated BBQ, close the lid and cook for 4-6 minutes, checking every 1-2 minutes.

GRILLED TUNA & SWEETCORN ON WHITE

Ingredients

2 slices of white bread

1 small tin of tuna (1 tin will make two sandwiches)

20g coriander

1 small red onion diced

Juice of 1 lime

2 tbspn. mayonnaise

1 small tin of sweetcorn (rinsed under cold water and strained)

Butter to spread on each slice (a small film is plenty)

20g grated Mozzarella cheese (you can also use Brie or Camembert but they're slightly more expensive)

Method

Heat the heavy based frying pan.

Whilst it's heating, mix the tuna with the mayonnaise, sweet corn, onion, lime juice, coriander and season.

Butter two slices of bread.

Place the desired amount of filling onto one of the slices on the non-buttered side.

Top with the second slice making sure the two sides exposed are the buttered ones.

Add to the pan and grill until golden on both sides.

This will take about 4-6 minutes.

Cut into twos or fours and serve with some side salad.

SERVES 1

When I first moved to Boston I was amazed at how popular grilled tuna and sweetcorn sandwiches were. But as the years passed I soon realised why. They are gorgeous and if you're lucky enough to come on some fresh Irish corn around September and October be sure to cook a batch, strip them and freeze to use over time. I'm blessed living in Longford as David Burns' Richmount Farm is only a few kilometres from Viewmount House so I get the best corn in the country direct to my door every season.

For this recipe though I'm going to use the corn from a small tin as they're available all year round. For any good grilled sandwich the key is to butter the outside of the bread and not the inside and secondly to use a good non-stick heavy-based pan.

Inset:
Gary and Netty on the Boston Duck Tour

GRILLED HAM, CHEESE & CHERRY PEPPER SANDWICH

Ingredients

2 slices bread (white or wheat)

2 slices of cheese of your choice - Brie, Cheddar or even Mozzarella works well

4 sweet cherry peppers sliced

3 slices crumbed ham

3 slices of onion

2 knobs of butter

SERVES 1

Method

Heat a heavy based non-stick frying pan.

Butter two slices of bread.

Add the ham, onion, cherry tomatoes and cheese to a non-buttered side.

Add the second slice of bread making sure the buttered slices are on the outside.

Add to the pan and grill until golden on both sides.

It's best to turn sides a few times and to heat slowly as it'll help you melt the cheese. If you use too high a temperature the bread will brown before the filling is hot.

You can jazz this up by using sourdough from a bakery or any type of speciality bread of your choosing.

Maybe add some crisp lettuce and tomato or even change the filling to cooked turkey or chicken.

Let your imagination go wild!

When it comes to a late night snack, my go-to dish is a grilled ham, cheese and cherry pepper sandwich. My brother Kevin and a group of friends recently came to stay with me. They didn't compliment me on the lovely dinner I spent hours cooking. Instead I got their attention with the late night sambos I rustled up. To keep them healthier, toast the bread. The filling combination works great together but for that added touch, lightly butter the bread and grill in a non-stick pan.

Inset:
Gary with his brother, Kevin

PAT'S MEAT PIE

(makes one 9-inch pie)

Ingredients

For the Pastry

200g butter

400g flour

Pinch of salt

95ml water

For the Filling

½ lb ground lean beef

½ lb ground pork

1 medium onion diced

½ tsp. salt

¼ tsp. pepper

¼ celery salt

¼ tsp. ground cloves

¼ tsp. cinnamon

¼ tsp. ground sage

¼ cup water or more (I also add a little of the fat from the meat after it is cooked)

Plain mashed potatoes (this I add by the consistency)⋆

⋆Usually takes about 6-8 potatoes, mashed without butter, milk or seasoning.

SERVES 6 

Method

Place the butter in a fridge then remove when cold and hard, dice. Add to a food processor with the flour and salt. Pulse for about 20 seconds until the dough is blended and crumb-like.

Add to a chilled bowl, make a well in the centre then add two thirds of the water. As the pastry gets closer to the correct consistency add the rest of the water, working with your fingertips.

Remove from the bowl, add a light dusting of flour to a work surface and knead your dough together.

When it has a soft texture like play dough it's ready. Wrap in cling film and let rest in the fridge for at least one hour. Remove, split in half and roll out to cover the baking tray.

Filling
Mix beef and pork, sauté with the chopped onion, add rest of ingredients to meat after cooking. When cooked you want the mixture to be dry. If it's still a little too wet just add a little more mashed potatoes.

Like every dish sometimes it's all about a little trial and error but trust me, this dish is worth the effort and before long you'll be making it without the need for a recipe.

Add the filling, then top with the pastry. Bake at 200°C for about 10 minutes then bring the temperature down to 180°C and continue cooking until golden and warmed through.

I first tasted 'Tourtiere' a traditional French Canadian Meat Pie on Christmas morning 2003. It was cooked by one of my closest friends and a cook with the best palate I've ever come across, Patricia Saiya. Over the years Pat, as we all know her, has made me two things that I'll never forget until the day I die. Her famous marinated bell peppers and her Meat Pie. Let's go back to Christmas Eve 2003. There's a mixture of Irish, American, Canadian and Italian in Pat's family and it's the Italian tradition of a seafood feast that brought me to Pat and Ray's house in Athol, west of Boston that day. It was a dinner I will never forget. One incredible seafood dish after another and before long my sadness at being away from home on Christmas Eve was slowly disappearing. What better place to be other than with my second family and enjoying some incredible food. The best though was still to come. Some families eat their meat pie at midnight on Christmas Eve, others Christmas morning. Our seafood dinner went on so long that it was to be Christmas morning before I got a taste of this famous meat pie. Pat has never given out this recipe to anyone outside her close family circle and so for that I am eternally grateful Pat. I've actually had the recipe for nine years now but the picture you see here in the book is my first attempt. Thank you Pat.

Inset:
Pat and Ray Saiya with Gary in Boston

TIME TO 2 IMPRESS

CULLEN SKINK

Ingredients

- 4 large fillets of smoked haddock, diced
- 4 white leeks, cleaned and diced
- 3 medium onions peeled and diced
- 2 litres of water
- 2 litres of heavy cream
- 4 chicken stock cubes
- 8 potatoes peeled and diced
- 500g flour
- 200-300ml vegetable oil
- Salt and white pepper to taste

Method

Add potatoes and onion to a large pot with the water.
Season with salt and pepper.

When boiling add the stock cubes.

When the potatoes are almost cooked add the leek.

Simmer for 10 minutes.

Mix the flour and oil together (you want a thick smooth roux).
If it’s too wet add flour and oil if it's too dry.

Slowly whisk in the roux until the water becomes very thick.
Be careful not to break up the potatoes.

The mixture needs to be thick enough so that when the cream is added the consistency comes back to where you need it.

Now add the cream followed by the diced Haddock.

Adjust the seasoning to personal taste.

The soup is supposed to be very thick - a proper winter warmer.

SERVES 8-10

This unique recipe is a thick chowder of Scottish origin using smoked haddock, potatoes and onions. This soup is a local specialty, from the town of Cullen in Moray, on the north-eastern coast of Scotland. The soup is often served as a starter at formal Scottish dinners. I first tasted Cullen Skink in The West Cork Hotel in September 2012 when I was attending the annual Celtic Cook Off which I went on to win, representing Ireland. On the night prior to the competition Chef Roy Brett of Ondine Edinburgh, the previous year's winner, made this dish as one of his courses for the champions dinner. I'll never forget it. It's the best chowder I've ever tasted and a dish that will live long in my memory. Here's my take on it. Serve with any of the crusty breads from this book.

**Inset:
Chef Roy Brett of Ondine Edinburgh**

NETTY'S FAVOURITE - CHICKEN SALAD MIX

Ingredients

1 chicken breast

1 lemon

Drizzle of olive oil

1 stalk of celery

1 tsp. chopped parsley

2 tbspn. mayonnaise

SERVES 2

Method

Heat the oil in a heavy based frying pan.

Season the chicken with salt and white pepper. Add to the pan.
Seal the chicken without browning too much.

Add the juice of half the lemon and place into a pre-heated oven at 180°C for 8 minutes.

Remove the chicken when cooked from the oven and place on a plate then into the fridge to cool completely.

Peel the tough back strands from the celery stalk then dice up as small as possible.

When cooled, remove the chicken from the fridge and dice up as small as possible.

Add the chicken, celery, mayonnaise, parsley and remaining lemon juice to a bowl and mix with a spoon.

Adjust seasoning and serve on an open sandwich, between two slices of bread or even in a wrap.

Or do what I do and just stuff it into your mouth with a spoon.

I like it acidic so I sometimes add a little extra lemon juice.

I got married in March 2013. Set in the incredible grounds of Viewmount House, I had planned seven plus courses of the finest food you could imagine. I was thinking, what course will they love the most? Will it be Anise Orange Cured Duck Leg Confit or Pig's Tail Croquettes with Yuzu Gel, Piquillo, Micro Cress and Pear Mustard? Maybe it'll be Salt Fried Sirloin Steak with Peppercorn Courvoisier Sauce, Colcannon & Straw Potatoes or the Dessert of Valrhona Chocolate Torte with Pear & Celery Ice Cream? No. The dish everyone talked about was the one I hadn't given a second thought to. It was about 4am and the poor DJ had finally stopped playing music and out rolled the sandwiches. I've always made chicken salad the same way but I never gave it much thought. Needless to say it has become a regular request from my wee wife Netty now on Sunday evenings whenever she's getting ready for school the next day. The mixture of lemon juice, mayo, celery and chicken gives this an addictive taste. Try it for yourself. You'll never make a chicken sandwich the old way again.

Inset:
Gary and Netty on their wedding day

LISSADELL MUSSELS
in Coconut Green Curry Broth
with Pineapple, Shiitake & Spring Onions

Ingredients

10 medium to large mussels (fully closed, de-bearded and washed)

1 shallot diced

1 clove of garlic crushed

⅛ of a fresh pineapple

½ cup shiitake mushroom

2 stalks of scallion

1 cup dry white wine

1 250ml tin of coconut milk

2 tbspn. Thai green curry paste

Salt and white pepper to taste

1 loose cup of fresh coriander (Thai basil is ideal but hard to find)

3 sprigs fresh mint

Crusty bread

Donegal rapeseed oil (Ireland's answer to olive oil)

SERVES 1

Method

Heat a heavy based frying pan with a little drizzle of Donegal rapeseed oil. Add the crushed garlic and shallots, sauté without colour until soft. Add the mussels and some seasoning, toss with the shallots and garlic then add the white wine.

Add a lid or invert an equal sized frying pan over the mussels to incorporate steam thus helping them to open.

Whilst the mussels are steaming mix the curry paste and coconut milk together, chop the fresh herbs and add half to the mix. Set aside. Season and taste (it's imperative to get your seasoning correct now and the level of spice you desire).

Now slice the scallions, dice the pineapple small and slice the shiitake mushrooms, being careful to slice around the tough centre piece of the mushroom and discard. Remove the lid, the mussels should be showing signs of opening. You don't want them to be fully open at this stage as they require more cooking time. Add the desired amount of coconut milk mixture (approximately enough to reach half depth of the mussel). Add the mushrooms and pineapple. Let the coconut broth come to the boil and reduce with the lid off. Once the mussels are fully opened and the sauce has now reduced to desired consistency, add in the scallions and remaining herbs. Toss the mussels in the broth so that they are all coated, and serve in a deep bowl. Top with some sliced crusty bread and drizzle on a little Donegal rapeseed oil. Serve with a lukewarm finger bowl with lemon and an empty bowl for shells.

I grew up in Ramelton and spent most summers walking the local shores searching for wild Donegal oysters, mussels and whelks. In my early career I'd often pair mussels with spicy tomato sauce and linguini or the classic way with white wine, lemon, garlic and parsley but this particular recipe has to be my all time favourite. Mussels take to spices very well and the combination of the coconut milk and the fruit add subtlety to the green curry paste. The key is to cut the ingredients up small enough that they find themselves falling into the shell so that each mussel takes on as many of the flavours as possible.

Inset:
Boat wreck at Ramelton Quay behind Conway's Bar

GUINNESS BREAD

Ingredients

250g flour
½ kg wholemeal flour
½ kg rye flour
450g treacle
250ml Guinness
2 tsp. salt
2 tsp. bi-carbonate of soda
100ml rapeseed oil or sunflower oil
Approximately 1 litre buttermilk

SERVES 8 per loaf

Method

Mix the treacle, oil and Guinness together and heat slightly so that the treacle emulsifies.

Then add the buttermilk.

Mix the dry ingredients together.

Add wet ingredients to dry, mix well.

Add to greased 2lb bread tins, about half way up.

Sprinkle with brown sugar.

Bake at 170°C for 30 minutes.

Turn them upside down in their tins and bake for a further 30 minutes.

Place on a cool rack for 20 minutes before slicing.

Makes approximately 4 tins.

TOP TIPS

The bread freezes well so don't be afraid to make the larger batch.

This is our most requested recipe in Viewmount House by a country mile. There isn't a night that someone doesn't ask for it so it's always at the ready to print out for any customer that fancies their chances at making it. It's extremely simple and without doubt, the nicest bread you'll ever eat. A bold statement yes! But make this and you'll see what I mean.

Inset: Chef Gary

WHITE BREAD, PARSLEY BREAD, WALNUT BREAD

Ingredients

200ml water

25ml olive oil

330g flour

6g salt

6g sugar

4g yeast

For Parsley Bread
add
30g chopped fresh parsley

For Walnut Bread
add
50g nibbed walnuts

For Egg Wash

2 eggs

200ml milk

SERVES 6-8 per loaf

Method

Soak the yeast in 100ml tepid water.
Leave in a warm place for about 5 minutes.

Sieve the flour, sugar and salt into a mixing bowl. Make a well in the centre and pour in the yeast mixture as well as the remaining water.

Mix the dough for about 5 minutes then cover with a clean kitchen towel and leave to rest for 5 minutes.

Knead for 5-10 minutes until smooth in the mixer.

Cover with cling film and leave for 1-1 ½ hours, then knock back and knead for 2-3 minutes. Leave to relax for 10 minutes.

Divide into two and split between two 1kg buttered bread tins.
Leave to prove until they double in size.

For the parsley bread and walnut bread brush with egg wash (2 eggs mixed with 200ml milk) but for the white bread just dust with flour.

Cook at 190°C for 15 minutes then remove from the tins and continue cooking for a further 5-10 minutes or until the bread sounds hollow when you knock the base.

Leave to cool on racks.

Anna Buchanan or Granny Tiger as I call her, gave me my very first memories of food. Anna was, and still is, the best baker I've ever met. The mother of my uncle-in-law Joe B, I found myself in her kitchen every weekend and during holidays as a child. I was never big enough to reach, or see over the counter top, but Anna used to make me stand on an up-turned pot or a stack of cookbooks in order to see what she was doing, and although I like to say I helped her I probably got in the way more than anything else.
Anna never weighed an ingredient so over the years I've tried to piece together her handfuls of this, pinches of that and cups of the other to try and recreate some of her gems.

Inset:
Gary with Anna Buchanan

FISH & SWEET POTATO CHIPS

Ingredients

1 8oz piece of fresh cod, haddock, whiting, plaice or sole

1 large sweet potato

Salt and pepper

300g self-raising flour

250ml sparkling water

1 tsp. chopped fresh thyme or parsley

Tartar Sauce

2 tbspn. mayonnaise

1 gherkin finely chopped

2 tsp. chopped capers

Juice of half a lemon

SERVES 1

TOP TIPS
For a healthier option bake or grill the fish and eliminate deep frying.

Method

For the Potato
Wash the sweet potato and peel. Cut in half lengthways. Cut each half into four wedges lengthways. Toss in a little olive or rapeseed oil, season with salt and pepper. Sprinkle with thyme and place in a pre-heated oven at 180°C. Bake until golden and a cocktail stick passes through the potato with little resistance.

For the Fish
Place the flour in a bowl. Add some salt and pepper. Add some sparkling water and whisk to the consistency of a thick milkshake. Season. Pass the fish through the batter mix. Do not pass the fish through flour before this step. This gives a lighter crispier batter. Drop into a pre-heated fat fryer at 170°C. After 10 seconds, give the fryer basket a light shake whilst the fish is submerged to lift the fish off the floor of the basket. This helps prevent the fish sticking to the basket. Once the fish floats you'll be sure it won't stick. Cook until it begins to brown and then lift the basket gently and leave it to drain and rest.

For the Sauce
Mix the mayonnaise, capers, gherkins and lemon juice together. Add the sweet potato wedges to the plate.

Drop the fish one last time and cook for approximately 2 minutes until golden and crispy. Lift out the fish and set on a kitchen paper towel to drain off excess oil. Add to the plate, spoon on a dollop of Tartar sauce. Serve with lemon wedges.

Most of us love fish and chips. A fresh piece of Irish flaky cod in crispy batter with a feed of mushy peas and fries is close to my food heaven. Growing up in Ramelton, Co. Donegal I loved when my father would bring back the brown paper bag filled with crispy whiting and chips from our local café, Steve's. It's still going to this day and in fact my mother now works there a few days a week. She loves the hustle and bustle of the café and when I'm at home in Ramelton from time to time she will take a bag of fish and chips home and it always brings back memories of trying to keep my eyes open late at night in the hope that when Daddy got in he might have some with him. My older brother Pearse and I would sneak out of bed and try not to wake up Cha, Kevin or Emma 'cause it meant more for us. This recipe is a slightly different version to Steve's classic but it's well worth a try.

Inset:
Gary with his brother, Pearse

Mains

From budget cooking with Fisherman's Pie, turning the humble sausage into an incredible meal with Ernan McGettigan's Pork sausages and a leftover meal using trimmings from Lamb Shoulder, this is a chapter where those of you who love tasty food without breaking the bank will be right at home.

Granny Hanlon's memorable Parsley Sauce gets paired with an old Irish favourite in Boiled Bacon. The dish that I pretty much thank for getting me a second date with my now wife Annette, Chicken Piccata, is there for you all to attempt and for those of you that want to splash out there is a cracking Roast Beef dish with Duck Fat Yorkies.

Don't miss the tip on the Yorkies though, NEVER open the oven when cooking Yorkies and when you think they are ready don't take them out, give them another 5 minutes to crispen up and be sure they won't collapse. I credit my good friend Gareth Galligan, Head Chef in The Olde Post Inn, Cavan for that one.

Happy cooking!

Chef Gary

Chef Gary

TIME TO 2 IMPRESS

ANISE ORANGE CURED DUCK LEG CONFIT with

Beetroot, Mushroom, Tarragon & Sherry Ragout

Ingredients

2 duck legs

Rock salt (coarse)

4 star anise

½ fresh orange

½ cup chopped fresh tarragon

1 large beetroot cooked and cooled

2 cups fresh / wild mushrooms

2 shots Bristol cream sherry

2 cups of cream

1 bulb of garlic

Duck fat (enough to submerge the legs when melted)

SERVES 2

Method

Rub the duck legs generously with rock salt. Press two star anise into the flesh end of each and divide the tarragon between both, rubbing all over the skin and flesh.

Slice the oranges and place the duck legs on top and refrigerate for at least 24 hours to cure.

Melt the duck fat and add the bulb of garlic. Submerge the duck legs in the fat and place in a pre-heated oven at 120°C.

Confit slowly for approximately 3 hours or until the meat begins to fall off the bone. Remove from the fat and set aside.

Heat a frying pan, add a little olive oil and add the chopped mushrooms, season.
Peel and dice the beetroot and add to the mushrooms.
When almost cooked, add chopped tarragon, de-glaze with sherry then add cream and reduce until desired consistency is reached. Season to taste.

Place the duck legs under a grill until crispy. Spoon the beetroot ragout evenly between two plates and top with the duck leg.

Drizzle with a little truffle oil if you have it to enhance the flavour even more.

Serve.

TURN
PAGE
FOR
HOW-TO
GUIDE

This is my all time favourite dish. All it needs is time. I first tasted Duck Leg Confit in Cookes Restaurant in Dublin many years ago. But it wasn't until my chefing days in Boston that I mastered the cure.
A perfect confit will only be achieved if the cure is right. You'll get the meat coming off the bone but unless you get the cure right you won't get the flavour, and for me, if you don't have flavour you have nothing. You get out of this dish, what you put in. This is as simple as cooking gets. It's just many little steps that when all put together will give you a dish you'll never forget.

ANISE ORANGE CURED DUCK LEG CONFIT

STEP 1
Rub the duck legs generously with rock salt.

STEP 2
Press two star anise into the flesh end of each.

STEP 3
Divide the tarragon between both, rubbing all over the skin and flesh.

STEP 4
Slice the oranges and place the duck legs on top and refrigerate for at least 24 hours to cure.

STEP 5
Melt the duck fat and add the bulb of garlic. Submerge the duck legs in the fat and place in a pre-heated oven at 120°C.

Confit slowly for approximately 3 hours or until the meat begins to fall off the bone.

TIME TO 2 IMPRESS

SIRLOIN STEAK with Red Onion Mustard Seed Compote, Crozier Bleu Gratin

Ingredients

2 aged sirloin steaks

Rock salt

Pepper

Compote

3 red onions

2 tbspns. mustard seeds

Dash of Worcester sauce

4 tbspn. red wine vinegar

Dash of Tabasco

2 tbspn. Heinz tomato ketchup

SERVES 2

TOP TIP

The firmer a steak becomes the more well cooked it is.

Method

For the Compote

Sauté onions until soft.

Add remaining ingredients and cook slowly making sure to mix every 3-4 minutes.

Season to taste.

For the Steak

Set at room temperature for at least 1 hour.

Heat a heavy based frying pan.

Rub rock salt onto the steak on both sides.

Fry on each side turning every 2 minutes until desired temp is reached (rare, medium rare, medium, medium well, well done).

Rest the steak for approximately 2 minutes on a plate prior to serving in order to allow juices to settle.

Top with a spoon of the red onion mustard seed compote and a slice of crozier bleu cheese.

Place under the grill to melt the cheese and serve.

TURN PAGE FOR HOW-TO GUIDE →

The key to a good steak is simple. Start with well-aged meat. Look for plenty of marbling (the little white streaks through the meat) as this is where your flavouring is going to come from. Of all the demonstrations I do around the country a perfectly cooked steak is always something people want to see. You can replace the onion mustard seed compote and bleu cheese with the more traditional peppercorn sauce if you prefer but it's something different for those of you who fancy a change.

RED ONION MUSTARD SEED COMPOTE

How to GUIDE

STEP 1

Sauté onions until soft.

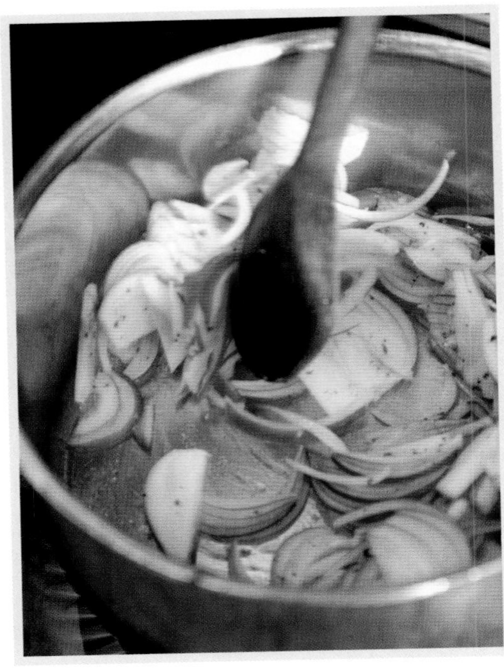

STEP 2

Add remaining ingredients and cook slowly making sure to mix every 3-4 minutes.

STEP 3

Season to taste.

HUNGRY AND 1 IN A HURRY

BRANDY PEPPERCORN SAUCE

Ingredients

4 tbsp. pink peppercorns

3 tbsp. cracked black pepper

2 tbsp. green peppercorns

1 onion, finely chopped

2 shots of brandy

1 chicken bouillon cube

250ml cream

500ml water

Bisto to thicken

Method

Smoke the peppercorns in a heavy based pot.

Add the onion and soften without colour.

Add the brandy, flambé.

Add the cream, bring to the boil then add the chicken bouillon cube.

Reduce the cream by half.

Now add the water, mix well.

Bring to the boil and thicken with the gravy mix.

Serve.

SERVES 4-6 (steaks)

Our steak recipe in the book has a red onion mustard seed compote with crozier bleu cheese. But for those of you who prefer the traditional peppercorn sauce here's a lovely recipe.
At Viewmount House we'll use reduced Veal stock as opposed to the Bisto of course. But not many of us have beef stock or veal stock to hand in our kitchen so you can use Bisto instead.

Inset:
Gary at Viewmount House

BRANDY PEPPERCORN SAUCE

How to GUIDE

STEP 1
Smoke the peppercorns in a heavy based pot.

STEP 2
Add the onion and soften without colour.

STEP 3
Add the brandy, flambé.

STEP 4
Add the cream, bring to the boil.

STEP 5
Add the chicken stock or Bisto mix and reduce by half.

STEP 6
Mix to incorporate the cream and gravy mix.

STEP 7
Simmer for 10-12 minutes.
Taste, season, serve.

WORTH THE 3 EFFORT

SLOW COOKED SHOULDER OF LAMB with Candied Swede, Boulangère Potatoes & Bordelaise

Ingredients

1 lamb shoulder boned, rolled and tied (your butcher will do this for you)

2 sprigs of rosemary

¼ cup of chopped thyme

5-6 litres chicken stock (alternatively dissolve 2 Erin chicken stock in 6 litres of boiling water)

½ bottle of red wine, ideally Merlot or Shiraz

1 parsnip and 1 carrot

1 large onion

Salt and pepper to taste

For Boulangère

6-7 potatoes sliced

1 large onion sliced

1 sprig rosemary chopped finely

4 sprigs of thyme chopped finely

Approximately 1 litre of chicken stock (reserved from the lamb ingredients)

2 knobs of butter

Candied Swede

½ turnip diced or cut into 3" rounds with a pastry cutter

4 tsp. honey

3-4 small slices of butter

Method

Heat a heavy based frying pan. Season the lamb all over and also the carrot, onion and parsnip. Sear the lamb all over to seal in the juices, lightly colour the vegetables. Sprinkle on the herbs. Place the vegetables onto a deep roasting tray and top with the lamb. Deglaze the pan with the red wine and pour over the lamb. Add the chicken stock reserving 1½ litres for the boulangère. Cover. Cook on a low heat for approximately 4-5 hours at 120°C or until the meat is very soft to touch and is breaking away easily when touched with a fork.

For Boulangère

Grease a casserole dish with the butter. Line with a layer of potatoes. Top with onion then some thyme and rosemary. Repeat finishing with a layer of potatoes and a little herbs. Add stock until you've almost reached the top of the potatoes. Cover with tinfoil. Oven cook at 160°C for approximately 45 minutes. Remove the foil for the last 10 minutes and raise the temp to 180°C to lightly brown and crust the top.

For Swede

Place your cut up swede on a baking sheet or casserole dish. Drizzle with honey and season with a little salt. Top with butter. Bake at 160°C for 45 minutes turning half way through. Serve.

For Bordelaise

Sauté the pearl onions. Add the red wine and reduce. Add 2 cups of the cooking liquor from the lamb and reduce until it's at desired consistency. Finish with chopped parsley.

I first made boulangère potatoes when I was 17 and working as a commis chef in Dublin. I worked with a few crazy English and French chefs and they loved boulangère potatoes. A lovely accompaniment to roast lamb, whether it's the leg or shoulder, you're on to a winner but for me the shoulder wins hands down. It's cheaper and although it takes longer to cook it's that low and slow method that's going to deliver the maximum amount of flavour. Enjoy.

Inset: Chef Gary

SLOW COOKED SHOULDER OF LAMB

How to GUIDE

STEP 1
Heat a heavy based frying pan. Season the lamb all over and also the carrot, onion and parsnip.

STEP 2
Place on the pre-heated pan.

STEP 3

Sear the lamb all over to seal in the juices, lightly colour the vegetables.

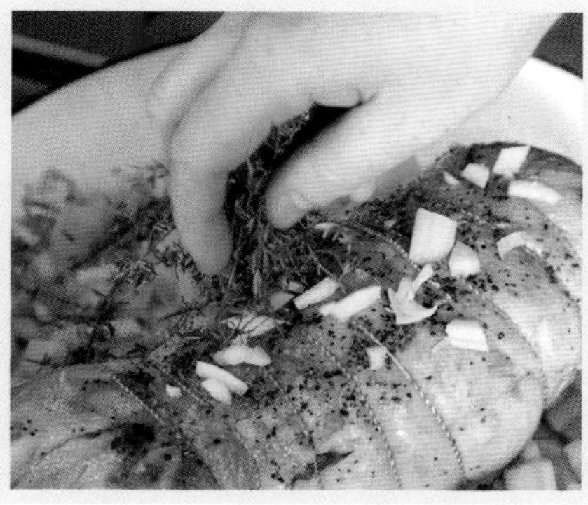

STEP 4

Place the vegetables onto a deep roasting tray and top with the lamb. Sprinkle on the herbs.

STEP 5

Deglaze the pan with red wine and pour over the lamb.

STEP 6

Add the chicken stock reserving 1½ litres for the boulangère. Cover. Cook on a low heat for approximately 4-5 hours at 120°C or until the meat is very soft to touch and is breaking away easily when touched with a fork.

TIME TO 2 IMPRESS

ROAST SIRLOIN OF AGED IRISH BEEF with Duck Fat Yorkies

Ingredients

2-3kg piece of Irish sirloin

2 carrots

2 onions roughly chopped

3 stalks of celery

2 bay leaves

Yorkies

500ml milk

500g flour

50g fresh time

3 eggs

Salt and pepper

500ml melted duck fat or vegetable oil

SERVES 8-10 

TOP TIP

Yorkshire Puddings:

Whenever you think they are ready, cook them for a further 5 minutes.

NEVER open the oven door during cooking.

Method

Pre-heat the oven to 180°C.
Heat a heavy based frying pan and sear the piece of beef on all sides to seal in the flavour. Add the vegetables to a roasting tray, place the piece of seared beef on top and roast for approximately 1 hour 10 minutes. This will cook the meat to medium. However, if you prefer it more well done, cook for a further 10-20 minutes.

Get a muffin tin and half fill each hole with duck fat and place in the oven.

Blend all the pudding ingredients together to the consistency of a light slow pouring batter. If it's too thick add a little milk or if it isn't thick enough add a little more flour.

Be careful when handling the tray of hot oil. Remove it from the oven when it's starting to smoke and pour your batter into the oil.
Fill them to the edges. Don't worry about the tray looking messy, just be careful none of the oil is spilling over the outer edges.

Place into the pre-heated oven and bake for about 20 minutes. **Do not open the door.** It's easier if your oven has a glass door to allow you to see.

One cooked, take the beef from the oven, cover with foil. Leave to rest for at least 20 minutes before slicing.

To make gravy simply reduce 200ml of red wine by half then strain the meat juices into it and pour over the beef and Yorkies. Season to taste.

TURN PAGE FOR HOW-TO GUIDE →

I'm blessed that John Stone Beef is close to Viewmount House and over the years I've struck up a great friendship with Allan Morris who runs the company and Marty his chief selector. They are two great guys with a huge passion for Irish Beef and a knowledge that's second to none. It's hugely important to create relationships with suppliers and likewise for you the consumer to develop one with a local butcher. Trust me when I say that your butcher always has a trump card hanging in a cold room not too far away from the counter for his favourite customers. Just ask him if he has any well-aged Sirloin with good marbling in stock and chances are he will. It can be a little expensive but for that special occasion Roast Sirloin of Aged Irish Beef is one that's worth going the extra mile for.

Inset:
Gary with Allan Morris of John Stone Beef (formerly Donald Russell) Photo by Paula Ryan Photography

DUCK FAT YORKIES

How to GUIDE

STEP 1

Pre-heat the oven to 180°C.
Get a muffin tin and half fill each hole with duck fat and place in the oven.

Blend all the pudding ingredients together to the consistency of a light slow pouring batter. If it's too thick add a little milk or if it isn't thick enough add a little more flour.

STEP 2

Be careful when handling the tray of hot oil. Remove it from the oven when it's starting to smoke and pour your batter into the oil. Fill them to the edge. Don't worry about the tray looking messy, just be careful none of the oil is spilling over the outer edges.

STEP 3

Place into the pre-heated oven and bake for about 20 minutes.
Do not open the door.
It's easier if your oven has a glass door to allow you to see.

TIME TO 2 IMPRESS

BANGERS 'N' MASH
with Onion & Grain Mustard Gravy

Ingredients

3 pork sausages

2 tsp. olive oil

1 small onion sliced

2 tsp. wholegrain mustard

3 tsp. Worcester sauce

1 tsp. Tabasco

50ml red wine vinegar

300ml water

2 tbsp. Bisto chicken granules

3 potatoes

1 knob butter

30ml milk

Salt and pepper to taste

SERVES 1

Method

Cover the potatoes with water.
Add salt and cook until tender.
Strain, add the milk, butter and a little salt.
Mash and set aside.

When the potatoes are half way there start the sausages.

Heat a heavy based frying pan.
Add the olive oil then the sausages.
Cook on a low heat until slightly golden all over.

Add the sliced onion and cook until the onions are soft but without colour.

Add the Tabasco, wholegrain mustard, Worcester sauce and red wine vinegar.

Cook until the vinegar reduces by half then add the water.

Turn up the heat and when the water comes to a simmer turn down and whisk in the Bisto chicken granules.

Simmer until it thickens and season to taste.

Serve over the mashed potatoes and sprinkle on some fresh parsley if you have some.

TURN PAGE FOR HOW-TO GUIDE →

I've two memories from my childhood that stand out. Both are from Granny Josie's house.
I remember drinking tea there. It's the only place I ever drank tea because Granny Josie let me put 10 spoons of sugar in it. My second memory is that she cooked the tastiest sausages. My grandfather Miles, God rest him, would always drive us home to Ramelton on a Sunday night after Glenroe. But not before we had Granny Josie's sausages. She started to cook them at the edge of the range an hour before the show and we'd eat them during it. The sausages were so soft and had charred edges. As I've grown older and life has become more hectic I rarely spend more than ten minutes cooking sausages. But from time to time when I really want to reminisce about those great days I make sure to stop in Donegal Town, grab some pork sausages from the master himself, Ernan McGettigan and shoot home to Ramelton to spark up a Bangers 'N' Mash. Here's my take on it. I hope it brings back some nice memories for you.

Inset:
Gary with Granny Josie

BANGERS 'N' MASH
with Onion & Grain Mustard Gravy

How to GUIDE

STEP 1
Heat a heavy based frying pan. Add the olive oil then the sausages. Cook on a low heat until slightly golden all over.

STEP 2
Add the sliced onion and cook until the onions are soft but without colour.

STEP 3

Add the Tabasco, wholegrain mustard, Worcester sauce and red wine vinegar.

STEP 4

Cook until the vinegar reduces by half then add the water.

STEP 5

Turn up the heat and when the water comes to a simmer turn down and whisk in the Bisto chicken granules.

STEP 6

Simmer until it thickens and season to taste.

TIME TO 2 IMPRESS

BOILED BACON with Cabbage, Champ & Parsley Sauce

Ingredients

1 small piece of bacon collar, approximately 1-2kg

4 medium potatoes

2 scallions

Knob of butter

50ml milk

Salt and white pepper

300ml milk

2 tbsp. cornflour

100g chopped parsley

1 medium onion roughly chopped

SERVES 2

Method

Boil the bacon for about 2 hours.
Set aside keeping warm.

Boil the peeled potatoes, strain and mash. Add the scallion, milk, butter and season to taste.

Bring 250ml of milk to the boil with the onion.

Mix the cornflour with the remaining 50ml of milk then whisk into the milk and onions.

Adjust the consistency then add the chopped parsley.

Season to taste.

Thinly slice some savoy cabbage then sauté in a little oil (or steam for a healthier option) for 12 minutes or until the leaves are soft.

Spoon the champ onto the plate.

Top with bacon and cabbage, then add the thick parsley cream sauce.

Believe it or not, Granny Hanlon always cooked dinner for my Grandfather Duncan before 11am in the morning. My Grandfather set out early to the marts around county Donegal. I used to time running over to Granny's from my Auntie Kate's house to coincide with these magic dinners then back to Kate's for dinner at 1pm. What can I say? I was a greedy little thing! But destined to be a Chef, I guess.

Sadly Duncan passed away long before his time and even though he christened me, 'The Bin' and 'Scarecrow' for stealing his dinners I, like all my family and Granny, miss him dearly.

This recipe however, comes from a dinner my Granny used to make for my uncle Anthony before he got married. It's boiled bacon, cabbage and champ with parsley sauce and I remember it fondly because of the parsley sauce. I usually make it with a roux at work but Granny insists it's all about the cornflour and the onions so I'm sticking with her version. A childhood memory I'll never forget thanks to Granny Hanlon.

Inset:
Gary with Granny Hanlon

CHICKEN PRIMAVERA
with Crème Fraîche & Bacon

Ingredients

Half a chicken breast sliced

1 slice of bacon

100ml white wine (optional)

1 clove of garlic crushed

30g red pepper

30g sliced onion

30g garden peas or frozen peas

30g courgette

3 tbsp. crème fraîche

Juice of 1 lime

Drizzle of olive oil

250g penne pasta

30g chopped fresh coriander

SERVES 2

Method

Boil a pot of salted water and add the penne pasta.

Cook until the pasta still has a little bite, al dente.

Heat a heavy based non-stick pan.
Add the oil and then the chicken.

Cook until golden, add the bacon and colour slightly.

Now add the garlic and cook for 30 seconds on a high heat.

Add the remaining vegetables but not the peas.

Add the lime juice and white wine.

Reduce by half and add the crème fraîche.

Reduce the crème fraîche until it thickens slightly then add the penne pasta and mix well.

Now add the peas and coriander and cook for a further 30 seconds to 1 minute.

Serve.

TURN PAGE FOR HOW-TO GUIDE →

It's not often my wife Netty cooks for me but when she does it's generally pretty good. She never really believes me though when I tell her I enjoy something but the truth be told most Chefs appreciate anything someone else cooks for them. It's nice to have the tables turned. This next dish is my little variation on the best meal Netty has ever made me. She cooked it one Sunday evening after a long hard week and it was heaven on a plate. Give it a go.

Inset:
Gary and Netty

CHICKEN PRIMAVERA
with Crème Fraîche & Bacon

How to GUIDE

STEP 1
Cook the pasta, al dente. Heat a heavy based non-stick pan. Add the oil and then the chicken.

STEP 2
Cook until golden, add the bacon and colour slightly.

STEP 3
Add the garlic. Cook for 30 seconds on a high heat. Add the remaining vegetables but not the peas.

STEP 4
Add the lime juice and white wine.

STEP 5

Reduce the wine by half and add the crème fraîche.

STEP 6

Reduce the crème fraîche until it thickens slightly.

STEP 7

Now add the peas...

STEP 8

...then add the penne pasta and mix well.

STEP 9

Now add the coriander and cook for a further 30 seconds to 1 minute. Serve.

HUNGRY AND 1 IN A HURRY

PENNE PASTA WITH A RAGOUT OF LAMB,

Chick Pea, Tomato & Courgette

Ingredients

Chop up remaining lamb from your roast

8oz penne pasta cooked, strained and kept warm

½ tin chickpeas

½ courgette diced

1 onion

Remaining herbs from the roast

1 tin chopped tomatoes

Salt and pepper

Method

Sauté the onion without colour and add the chopped tomatoes, then the herbs and cook slowly for 30 minutes.

Set aside.

Now sauté the chickpeas and courgette without colour.

Add the lamb and season, then add the tomato sauce.

Mix slowly and add a little of the remaining cooking liquor from the roast if needed.

Spoon the pasta into serving bowls and top with the ragout.

Alternatively you can add the pasta to the pan and toss all the ingredients together before serving.

SERVES 2

This is the perfect recipe for using up leftover roast lamb leg or lamb shoulder. If anything the flavour of the lamb will be even more intense on day two or three, so you'll be left with a robust, full flavoured dish that costs pennies.

WORTH THE 3 EFFORT

BRAISED LAMB SHANK
with Root Vegetable Espagnole

Ingredients

1 lamb shank
1 carrot
1 onion
1 celery stalk
2 cloves of garlic
5 sprigs of thyme
1 tin of chopped tomatoes
4 tsp. tomato puree
1 parsnip
250ml white wine
Water to cover

For the Gremolata

1 clove garlic chopped
1 tsp. grated lemon zest
1 tsp. chopped parsley

Mix all together

SERVES 1

Method

Heat an oven-ready casserole dish with a little oil.
Season the shank all over and sear until dark brown all over.

Roughly chop up all the vegetables and add.
Now add the chopped garlic and cook for 2 minutes.
Add the wine and reduce by half.
Add the tomato puree and mix in.

Now the chopped tomatoes and cover the shank with water.

Put the lid on the casserole dish and place in a pre-heated oven at 150°C to braise for approximately 3 hours or until the meat starts to come away from the bone easily.

Serve with mashed potatoes, risotto or roasties and sprinkle on a little of the gremolata to finish.

TOP TIP

This recipe serves one.
Simply add an extra shank per person.
The quantities of tomato puree and chopped tomato are the same even if you're cooking three or four shanks.
If you add any more than three use a little more carrot, onion and celery and then a touch more chopped tomato.

This is a perfect winter warmer. That's what I think of when I hear lamb shank. This dish melts in the mouth and is gorgeous. Simple to make, all you need is time. The hardest part of this dish is sitting around as the incredible smells of the shank braising waft through the house. Serve with anything from risotto to roast potatoes but my favourite way is always with mashed potatoes. Top with a little gremolata to lighten the flavour and the chances are you'll be using bread or a spoon to scoop up every last morsel of sauce left in the bowl.

Inset: Chef Gary

CELERIAC LASAGNA

TIME TO 2 IMPRESS

Ingredients

3 slices of celeriac (1cm thick discs from a whole peeled celeriac)

1 tin of chopped tomatoes

2 cloves garlic

1 tsp. thyme

40g red pepper

30g green pepper

100ml white wine

30g courgette

Olive oil

6 basil leaves

½ small white onion

2 tsp. tomato puree

30g mild white Cheddar cheese

Salt and pepper to taste

SERVES 1

Method

For the Celeriac

Cover the celeriac with water, add 2 tsp. of salt and bring to the boil. Simmer until a cocktail stick can go through the celeriac with a little resistance. Set aside.

For the Sauce

Chop the onion and garlic.
Heat a heavy based pot. Add a little drizzle of olive oil then the chopped onion and crushed garlic. Season.
Sweat without colour then add the chopped thyme and white wine.

Reduce by half and whisk in the tomato puree. Now add a small tin (150g) of chopped tomatoes. Cook slowly for approximately 50 minutes. Remove from the heat and add the freshly chopped basil.

Heat some olive oil in a heavy based pot. Dice up the courgette and peppers and sweat without colour. When seared but not fully cooked, add in some sauce and fold. Adjust seasoning to taste.

On a baking tray sprinkle some grated Cheddar or Irish Brie on each slice of celeriac. Bake until the cheese melts. Remove.

To plate add one disc of celeriac to a hot plate, top with some of the vegetable provencal mixture, then another disc of celeriac and repeat. Make sure you keep your best disc of celeriac for the top layer.

Serve and enjoy.

Inset: Chef Gary

GARY'S HOISIN CHICKEN
with Egg Noodles, Cherry Peppers and Cashew Nuts

Ingredients

1 7oz chicken breast, sliced

4 tbspn. hoisin sauce

4 tbspn. coconut milk

50g beansprouts

4 water chestnuts

10 slices bamboo shoots

4 cherry peppers, sliced (peppadew peppers)

1 garlic clove crushed

½ a shallot finely diced

Drizzle of olive oil

10 cashew nuts, roughly chopped

1 scallion finely sliced

½ small white onion, sliced

2 discs of dried egg noodles

½ bunch fresh coriander

Salt and pepper

Method

Cover the noodles with boiling water and set aside until soft.

Drain and set aside when soft.

Heat a heavy based non-stick frying pan and season.
Sauté the chicken, browning on all sides.
Add the shallots and garlic and cook until soft.

Add the cherry peppers, onions, peppadew peppers, water chestnuts and bamboo shoots.

Cook until soft then add the coconut milk and hoisin sauce.

Mix well and continue to cook for approximately 4 minutes.

Now add the cooked noodles then the beansprouts and toss in the sauce well.

Serve in a bowl topped with cashew nuts, scallion and fresh coriander.

SERVES 4

I first tasted hoisin sauce in South Beach Miami back in 2004. I was hooked. It was in a lovely little noodle and mixed vegetable dish and it's something I tend to have in the house now at all times. It works really well with chicken and because it tends to have a strong taste I usually cut it with coconut milk. It has a lovely subtle sweet flavour and takes well to spice also.

Inset:
South Beach, Miami, Florida, USA.

HUNGRY AND 1 IN A HURRY

CHICKEN PICCATA with

Broccoli, Baby Potatoes and Flat Parsley

Ingredients

For Piccata

2 chicken breasts butterflied and batted out thin

Juice of 1 lemon

1 cup loose flat parsley roughly chopped

3 tbspn. of mini capers

and 2 tbspn. of the caper juice

½ cup flour

Drizzle of rapeseed oil

½ pint of dry white wine

4/5 knobs of butter

Salt and pepper to taste

For the Baby Potatoes

8 baby potatoes

Salt and pepper

Splash of olive oil

Garnish

6 florets of broccoli

SERVES 2

Method

For the Potatoes
Boil the potatoes in salted water. Drain, heat the olive oil and sauté until golden, set aside.

Garnish
Par boil the broccoli, blanch and set aside for when the chicken is cooked.

For the Chicken
Add half the lemon juice, a little oil and ¼ of the parsley to the chicken and rub in and leave to marinate for approximately 1-2 hours.
Heat a heavy based frying pan and add some rapeseed oil or vegetable oil (olive oil is a little too strong). Season the chicken well and pass through the flour to get an even coating all over and add to the pan. Turn after 2-3 minutes and cook on the opposite side for 2 minutes. Now add the remaining lemon juice, capers and their juices and the white wine.
Turn the heat up high and reduce until you've half the quantity of wine left. Now add the knobs of butter one by one and toss the pan back and forth to create a wave and this folds the butter into the sauce and thus thickening it a little and giving it a beautiful rich glaze. Add the remaining parsley and toss one last time.

To plate, just spoon the potatoes into a wide bowl or plate. Top with the chicken and spoon over some sauce then arrange some broccoli around the plate.
Serve and enjoy.

This is one of my all time favourite dishes. This is the first thing I ever cooked for my wife Netty. This was my trump card. How could she not want to marry a man that could cook this wee gem? And I was right. In this recipe I serve it with baby potatoes but it's equally beautiful with champ or pasta.

Inset:
Gary and Netty on the day they got engaged

FISHERMAN'S PIE

TIME TO 2 IMPRESS

Ingredients

For the Sauce

450ml milk

40g butter

30-40g flour

¼ sliced white onion

1 bay leaf

Salt and white pepper

6 peppercorns

2 carrots diced

2 celery stalks peeled and diced

1 onion chopped

100g sweetcorn

Potato Crust

6-8 medium sized rooster potatoes

2 knobs butter

2 eggs

Salt and pepper

Seafood*

1 x 6oz piece of salmon (skinless and boneless)

1 x 6oz piece of cod (skinless and boneless)

6oz hand-picked white crab meat (this can be bought frozen so just defrost, check for shell and set aside)

6oz smoked haddock (optional, use any other non-smoked fish if you don't like the smoky flavour)

12 shelled Dublin Bay prawns

8oz monkfish tail cut up into ½ inch pieces

SERVES 6-8

TOP TIP

* This is the seafood that I would use but on any given day it depends on what I have in stock or in the freezer. There are no rules on the filling. Just use up whatever seafood you have or the cheapest pieces your fishmonger has for sale. The pie will be beautiful regardless of what goes inside.

We all get a kick out of being frugal with food. At least I do, and there is no better dish for using up little bits and pieces of seafood than this. As the weeks and months go by and you find yourself buying fish and cutting it up into portions you'll find you're always left with tail ends or small pieces that are just too small to cook or serve as a portion.

Don't throw them out. Cover with cling film, add a little sticky label with what it is and the date, freeze and when you've enough gathered up this pie is the dinner party cracker you're going to cook. It'll feed 6-8 people easily and it'll cost you pennies.

Inset: Chef Gary

FISHERMAN'S PIE

TIME TO 2 IMPRESS

Method

Half the potatoes and cover with cold water. Add salt and bring to the boil. When soft, remove and strain. Place back on the heat and shake the pot to help dry out the potatoes. Add the butter, season with salt and white pepper and mash. Taste, adjust seasoning and set aside.

For the Sauce
Add the milk, peppercorns, onion and bay leaf to a pot. Bring it to a boil, keeping a very close eye on it so that it doesn't boil over the pot. When it reaches this point, remove from the stove. Melt the butter in a heavy based pot, add the carrot, celery and chopped onion.
Add the flour and mix well. To prevent the roux going brown, don't use too high a heat. Let the roux cook out on a very low heat for 5 minutes. Now strain the milk mix into the roux and whisk well but avoid breaking the vegetables. Continue to cook on a low heat for 30 minutes mixing continuously or until the carrots and celery are cooked.
It's important that the sauce is quite thick. When the seafood is eventually added the moisture coming from the fish will thin the sauce slightly, so having the mixture that little bit thicker will mean that your finished pie won't be weak and watery.

For the Seafood
Cut up all the raw seafood into similar sized pieces. Place on a baking tray and bake in a pre-heated oven at 160°C for 5 minutes. Do not bake prawns, crabmeat or mussel meat if using these. Simply set them aside for the next step.

Add all the seafood to a heavy based casserole dish.
Using a strainer scoop out as many vegetables as possible from the sauce-pot. Add in prawns, crabmeat and mussel meat if you're using. Give it a light fold or mix to spread the various different pieces of seafood around the pot.

Now pour in some more sauce but only enough to just about cover the filling. Make sure to leave a 2-inch gap in the dish for potatoes. Now spoon on the potato mix.

Mix the eggs with a fork and brush over the top of the potatoes then place in a pre-heated oven at 180°C for 12 minutes or until the crust is golden. Alternatively if you have a grill setting just put it up to max temperature, place your casserole dish under the heat and leave until a golden brown crust is reached.

Chef Gary

Desserts

Everyone loves desserts.

In this chapter, I re-visit my childhood love affair with Crunchie bars with my own version of Honeycomb and it's paired with chocolate sauce. There is the Sunday lunch favourite of Meringue Roulade and the simplest dessert of all time, Eton Mess.

For me though the winner of this chapter has got to be the Berrymisiu. On a hot day in Boston many moons ago I had a craving for a Tiramisu-like dessert but the ingredients associated with a Tiramisu just seemed too heavy for a summer's day so I decided to play around with different flavours whilst adding in summer berries. And so a new dessert was born. This dessert is a must try in the summer months but if you can get your hands on some berries during the autumn or winter why not give it a go.

Happy cooking!

Chef Gary

Chef Gary

MIXED BERRY ETON MESS

Ingredients

1 meringue nest
(store bought is fine or one you made yourself)

6 raspberries
4 strawberries
6 blueberries
6 blackberries

200ml cream

The scrapings of half a vanilla pod or 1 drop of vanilla essence

Method

Add the vanilla bean to the cream and whip to stiff peak.

Add the cream to a bowl and break the meringue on top.

Cut up the strawberries and add along with all the remaining berries.

Keep the rest whole.

Using a spoon mix the ingredients together gently.

Spoon into a glass or bowl and serve.

* Simply add a little extra fruit and meringue to feed some friends
* The cream quantity should be enough for 3-4 portions

SERVES 1*

When all else fails and you simply cannot get your head around making desserts, this is the one for you. If you can whip cream you can make this. For those of you that have tried the meringue roulade in the book you'll have no problems with this one. In fact, you'll be able to keep all the little broken up pieces of meringue and use them in this. An English classic that traditionally is made with strawberries it was served at Eton College at the annual cricket game against the pupils of Harrow School.

Bananas were also used and in fact initially it was made without meringue but that came about around the 1970's.

As I often say, there are no rules in cooking. If you want to put your own little twist on things always feel free to do so. If you have any fruit left over or about to go off simply pick up some cream, meringue nests and away you go. It can be strawberry Eton mess, banana Eton mess, blackberry Eton mess or simply 'everything I found sweet in my fridge' Eton mess.

HONEYCOMB
with Chocolate Sauce

Ingredients

Honeycomb

200g caster sugar

50ml water

50ml honey

1 tbsp. liquid glucose

1 tsp. bicarbonate of soda

Chocolate Sauce

115g caster sugar

60ml water

175g plain chocolate (55%)

30g unsalted butter

30ml brandy

SERVES 8-10

Method

Honeycomb Method

Place the sugar, honey, glucose and water in a pot and using a sugar thermometer bring to 160°C.

Line a deep tray with parchment paper.

Once the mixture hits 160°C add the bicarbonate of soda whisking continuously.

This is when you need to be very careful with the mix as it'll begin to rise and bubble.

As it rises pour into the parchment-lined dish.

Leave to cool then break up into chunks.

Chocolate Sauce Method

Place the sugar and water in a pot and heat until the sugar dissolves.

Stir in the chocolate until melted then add the remaining ingredients.
DO NOT bring it to the boil.

Add brandy.

It's ready to serve.

You can serve at room temperature or simply pour over the chunks of honeycomb and serve with ice cream.

"Thank Crunchie it's Friday." As a kid I grew up with those words ringing in my ears and to this day it's still one of my favourite chocolate bars. It was a momentous day the day I made honeycomb for the first time as a young commis Chef. As Irish people we have a love affair with honeycomb. Regardless of what dessert you put on the menu the one with honeycomb will almost always be the most popular. Here is a beautiful simple recipe with warm chocolate sauce for you to try. Like all caramels be careful with the mixture because as you work it, you'll be heating it to 160ºC.

Inset:
Gary with his siblings

RASPBERRY MARSHMALLOWS

Ingredients

250g granulated sugar

100ml water

60g glucose

3 egg whites

7 sheets gelatin

1 tsp. vanilla extract

2 punnets of raspberries or approximately 25 raspberries

SERVES 8-10

Method

Add sugar, glucose and water to a heavy based pot and boil until it reaches 127°C.

Soak the gelatin in cold water.
Beat the egg whites until stiff.

When the mixture is up to temperature carefully add in the gelatin. Bubble up. Pour into a jug.

Add the vanilla to the egg then pour the hot syrup in.

Continue whisking until the mixture is thick and is able to hold on to the end of the whisk.

Lightly oil a shallow tray (30cm x 20cm) Dust it with sieved cornflour and icing sugar.

Pour in half the mixture and even it out with a hot wet palette knife.

Add the raspberries then pour in the remaining half of the mixture.
Smooth over again.

Dust the top with cornflour and icing sugar then leave to set for at least an hour

Cut into cubes and serve.

Everyone deserves a little treat now and again and marshmallows are always a crowd favourite. They are perfect with some chocolate sauce or stick a little metal skewer through them and toast over an open flame to make them gooey. Stick them between two sweet wafers and you've got that eye-closing sweet treat that we all crave at some point.

For mine I've added some fresh raspberries from the Viewmount House gardens. Get out walking on the Irish country roads when they are in season and try them for yourself or alternatively add whatever fresh berries you come across. Blueberries, strawberries or blackberries are equally as good.

Inset: Chef Gary

STRAWBERRY MASCARPONE TARTLETS

Ingredients

Pastry
250g flour

200g unsalted butter

100g icing sugar

2 egg yolks

Pinch of salt

Filling
250g mascarpone cheese

100g fresh cream

150g condensed milk

1 vanilla pod scraped

5-7 small strawberries per tartlet

Extras
2 tbspn. apricot glaze

SERVES 6-8

Method

In a mixing bowl add flour, salt, icing sugar and butter and mix until it crumbles.
Then add the egg yolk and mix for approximately 1 minute until it comes together.
Remove from the bowl, set it on parchment paper.
Wrap it up and place into the fridge for at least 30 minutes.

Cut your pieces off the main batch and roll out to cover your desired tartlet mould.
Place the rolled-out dough over your moulds.
Press evenly into the sides and base then place in a pre-heated oven at 170°C and bake until golden for approximately 9 minutes.

For the Filling

Mix all the ingredients together in a mixing bowl.

Add the mix to a piping bag and squeeze into the cooled tartlets.

If you don't have a piping bag simply spoon the mixture into the tartlets.
Top with sliced or quartered strawberries then brush on a little apricot jam.
Take two spoons of apricot jam, melt in a microwave then brush over the strawberries to bring up a sheen.

Dust with icing sugar.
Serve.

This is a perfect summer afternoon tea dish. These beautiful wild strawberry and mascarpone tartlets are sure to be a hit with all guests.

They are small, light and delicate and are perfect when the sun shines. Strawberries can pretty much be bought now all year round in Ireland but if you can, hold out until the wild Irish gems appear. They are easy to grow in pots or if you don't have green fingers you're sure to pass a little strawberry hut near your home during the summer months.

BERRYMISIU

Ingredients

Cooked sponge (1 sheet)

Syrup from one tin of peaches, fruit cocktail or pears

1 lemon

1 small tub of mascarpone cheese

¾ spoons icing sugar

¾ drops vanilla essence or 1 pod, seeds scraped out

2 cups fresh berries, strawberries, blackberries, raspberries and redcurrants

2 spoons caster sugar

4 or 5 spoons crème de cassis

½ litre whipped cream

SERVES 4-6

Method

Mix the cheese, icing sugar and vanilla together until mixture is creamy.

Fold in the whipped cream.

Mix the berries with the caster sugar and set aside.

Place the sponge into the bottom of the desired amount of glasses.

Mix the crème de cassis, lemon juice and syrup from the tinned fruit together.

Pour stock syrup into the glasses over the sponge, enough to soak.

Add a spoon of berries and then some cheese mixture.

Repeat the process twice more, then top with a nest of the cheese and add a spoon of berries to the centre.

Serve.

This is my twist on the classic Tiramisu. I replace the usual coffee and coffee liqueur with some fruity crème de cassis and I incorporate some fresh berries. This is the perfect treat on that rare sunny day.

MERINGUE ROULADE
with Fresh Fruits & Cream

Ingredients

Meringue
6 large egg whites
250g caster sugar

Cream
500ml whipping cream
2 drops vanilla essence

Fruit Salad
12 strawberries, quartered

1 kiwi, diced

The segments of 2 mandarins

2 sliced bananas

50g blueberries

12 blackberries

100g pineapples

Half a ripe nectarine cubed

SERVES 8-10

Method

Add the egg whites to a large bowl and mix on a low speed for approximately 2 minutes. When it begins to foam turn up to a medium speed.

Keep beating until the egg whites stiffen. Then turn up to a high speed as you gradually add the caster sugar. Beat until glossy.

Line a baking tray with parchment paper.

Spoon the meringue onto the parchment-lined baking sheet and spread out the meringue in an even thin layer.

Place into a pre-heated oven at 110°C and bake for one hour.

Turn the oven off, leaving the meringue sheet inside. When the oven cools you can remove. It should be fully dried.

Whip the cream and vanilla together until stiff. Spread onto the meringue sheet leaving a one-inch piece of cream free all around the edges.

Spoon the fruit along the first one third of the sheet closest to you.

With the help of the parchment paper lift up the edge closest to you and flip it over the line of fruit. Tuck it in and roll it out all the way tucking the fruit into the middle.

Slice into desired portions. Serve.

One sheet will feed 8-10 adults.

This is the ultimate Sunday lunch dessert. It's full of fruit and fresh cream, then wrapped in addictive meringue. What's not to love about a fresh fruit meringue roulade?
This is probably not a dessert you would make for one, but it's certainly ideal for a gathering of family or friends. All the work can be done a day ahead of your special event and all that's left to do on the day is to make a bowl of fruit salad, whip some cream and assemble.

Inset: Chef Gary

MERINGUE ROULADE
with Fresh Fruits & Cream

STEP 1
Whip the cream and vanilla together until stiff.

STEP 2
Spread onto the meringue sheet leaving a one-inch piece of cream free all around the edges. Make sure the meringue sheet is sitting on a sheet of parchment paper, otherwise you'll be in bother when you go to roll it.

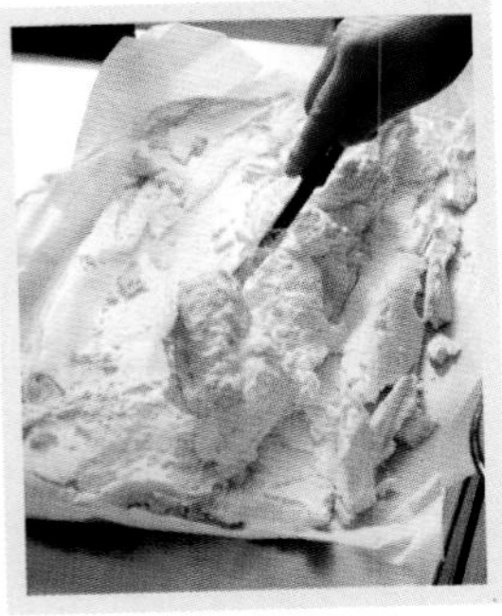

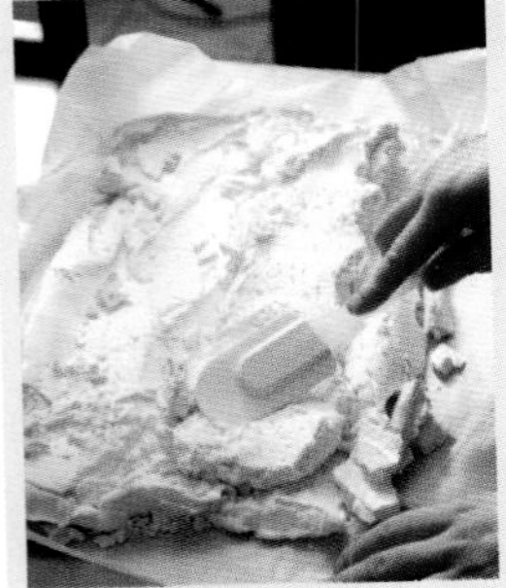

STEP 3

Spoon the fruit along the first one third of the sheet closest to you.

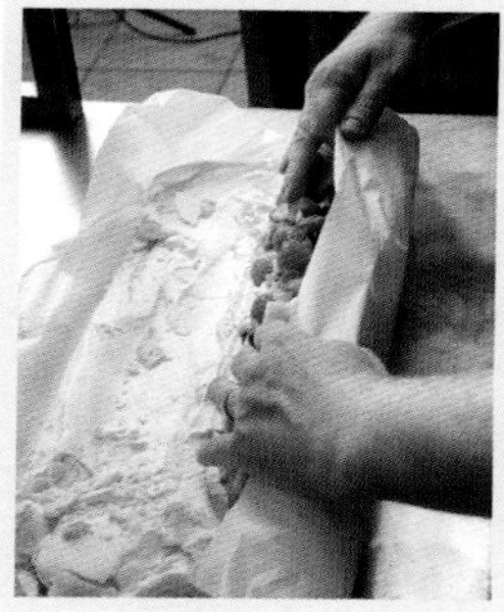
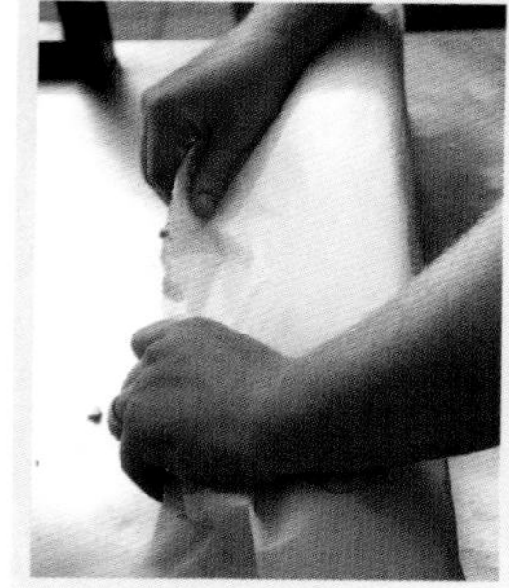
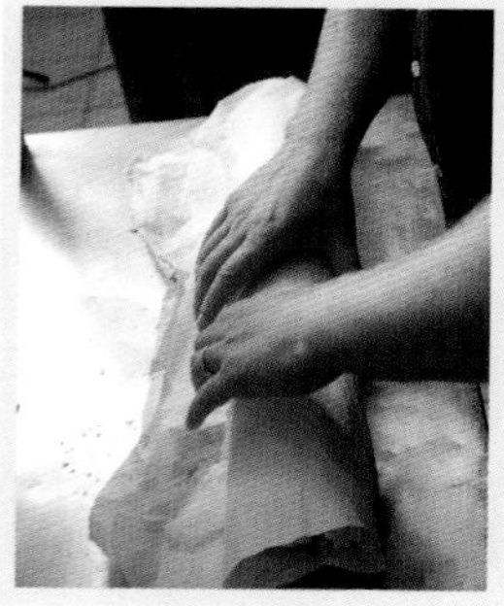

STEP 4

With the help of the parchment paper lift up the edge closest to you and flip it over the line of fruit. Tuck it in and roll it out all the way tucking the fruit into the middle.

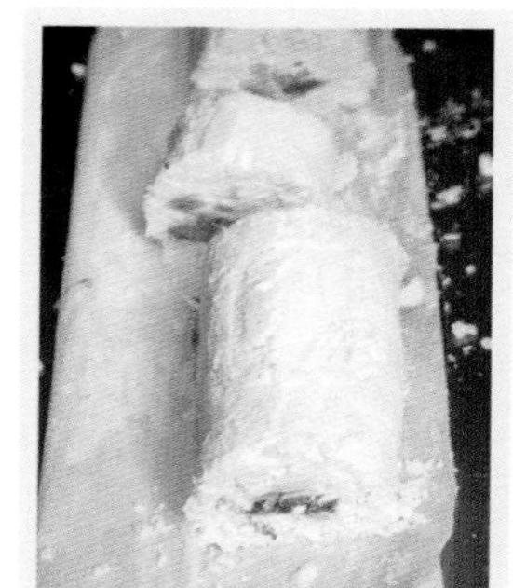

STEP 5

Slice into desired portions. Serve.
One sheet will feed 8-10 adults.

Index

K

L

M

N

O

P

Q

R

S

V

W

Y

Notes

Bluebird Care Ireland provides quality home care and independent living support services in the home and community setting. We work with people of all ages and varying degrees of ability.

Our company meets the physical, intellectual and emotional needs of our customers and their families. We are dedicated to providing these services in a highly professional and dignified manner, in a positive atmosphere while ensuring value for money.

We excel at high-quality care delivery and management vis-à-vis our commitment to external quality standards and internal quality audits. This is also reflected in our nationwide Q Mark Standard for home care services.

Bluebird Care has 20 offices nationwide. Find your local Bluebird Care office by contacting us in the following ways:

Don't forget you can watch videos of Gary O'Hanlon cooking recipes from Food for the Soul on our YouTube Channel and on our website.